the me
WITHOUT

A Year Exploring
Habit, Healing, and Happiness

Jacqueline Raposo

ixia
PRESS

Mineola, New York

Bibliographical Note

The Me, Without: A Year Exploring Habit, Healing, and Happiness
is a new work, first published by Ixia Press in 2019.

Library of Congress Cataloging-in-Publication Data

Names: Raposo, Jacqueline, author.
Title: The me, without : a year exploring habit, healing, and happiness /
    Jacqueline Raposo.
Description: Mineola, New York : Ixia Press, [2019] | Includes
    bibliographical references.
Identifiers: LCCN 2018032079| ISBN 9780486826882 | ISBN 0486826880
Subjects: LCSH: Habit breaking. | Change (Psychology) | Happiness. |
    Self-realization.
Classification: LCC BF337.B74 R37 2019 | DDC 158.1—dc23
LC record available at https://lccn.loc.gov/2018032079

Ixia Press
An imprint of Dover Publications, Inc.

Manufactured in the United States by LSC Communications
82688001   2018
www.doverpublications.com/ixiapress

For Lyndsey Ellis,
you are my scarlet cathedral.

CONTENTS

I think I'm happy.
Or otherwise distracted.
Don't try to trap me
with an offer more attractive.
Were you not impressed?
I've had to go through hell.
I used to be depressed.
I think that all is well.
It's still too early to tell.

Robbie Gil, *Happy?*

AN INVITATION

This book is a recording of a path.

It contains mostly memoir.

Some popular psychology. Neurology.

Some nerdy history and literature.

And some straight-up hippie love talk.

I interview engineers, professors, and designers.

A tarot reader, a podcast host.

(I flip cards and host my own show too.)

I quote Lorelai Gilmore.*

I accidentally quote musicians I'm not cool enough to know I'm quoting.

The path is messy because I am a human, and humans are messy.

But it has direction because this is a book, and books require direction.

It's full of self-contradiction.

Because sometimes experience inspires our truth to change.

Thank you for joining me.

(*Copper boom.)

A PROLOGUE

June 2016, I had lost *it*.

I didn't know what *it* was. But *it* had fled.

My path. My passion. My purpose.

My juju. My life force. *Whatever*.

Gone.

Nothing had happened, per se. Life was kosher.

I was fine.

I was *fine*!

I was a fine person, relatively speaking too.

I tried to be good and kind to friend and stranger alike. I recycled and donated a bit above the norm. I passed as a middling successful food writer and lifestyle podcast host. I spent time with my family and supported my friends. I managed my work/life schedule from the comfort of my uptown Manhattan apartment. (Well, *way* uptown. The hood Lin-Manuel Miranda sang about long before *Hamilton*.)

I didn't have a closet of Manolos or anything. But life was fine.

I should have been *happy*.

Period.

But I was . . . *happy*?

Question mark?

Memory's a funny thing. Now, way out of my comfort zone as I process and condense this sliver of my life, I think back and clearly see how I spent years justifying *happy*? by doing what we're told to do and obsessively recounting blessings: I *have work that brings creative satisfaction. I have a safe apartment with a compatible roommate and a desk by a window with a view of street and sky. I have a family I enjoy and love. I have Mitra, the best soulmate dog who ever fetched. I have devoted friends. I am healthy enough to hold my job.*

Yes. At the start of this story, I wanted *happy. period.*

But complacency muddled how things in my life were so very *bad.*

Career stumbling blocks had shriveled my creative confidence. Although overworking to increase my income, I kept falling further into debt. Hosting a dating podcast should have had me at the front of the pack, yet I hadn't shared deep romantic love in years. And despite decades of investment in my health, my chronic illness kept worsening and I couldn't seem to stop it.

I couldn't seem to better *any* of it.

I'd overhauled my career in workshops and networking groups.

I'd put my physical faith in doctors and alternative practices.

I'd dropped dreams and dollars, harvesting happy.

And still, I wandered in a fog I couldn't identify or outmaneuver.

At night, I'd slowly pace Riverside Drive, alone but for Mitra, oblivious with her nose to the ground. The romantic haze of orange streetlamps cast shadows from tall stone buildings down on to the wide expanse of street. Night after night I ambled, up and down, my songwriter friend Robbie Gil's voice on repeat in my ears, underscoring like a soundtrack:

"I think I'm happy. Or otherwise distracted . . ."

And then one day, I cracked.

CHAPTER
CHALLENGE **I**

NO SOCIAL MEDIA

UNPLUGGED

June 20, I go on to *Love Bites Radio* and blame the Internet.

"I'm sick of it!" I rebel-yell at my cohost and best man-bud, Ben, live on the air. I blame social media and dating apps, specifically, shaming the addictive technology I decide *must* be the reason why I can't see through the fog. I have no idea where I'm going with this yet. But I can't tolerate the status quo any longer. And so I make a brash and definitive declaration:

Tomorrow, I will quit online social stuff for a biblical forty days.

"I'm like a circa-twenty-first-century Jesus!" I cackle.

(I may have wine in hand.)

Ben calls bullshit.

He reminds our audience that I've similarly sworn off dating apps in the past, only to return twenty-four hours later. (Hey, a girl gets antsy.) And that I'm the one who forces him into many a selfie for the sake of promoting our "platform." But then he asks in kind sincerity, "What's *really* behind this?"

1

A neon On the Air glow grants time for nothing but a gut response. "It's a bunch of little things," I admit, increasingly vulnerable and unsure. "It's feeling disconnected as a human being?"

Ben and I started Love Bites a year ago, hoping a weekly public check-in might keep us active on the often-cutthroat thirty-something dating scene. For our audience (and ourselves), we test dating algorithms and online apps, interview relationship success stories, and coach each other from first dinner date through final breakup conversation. But while my time commitment to finding a mate online has increased, so has my frustration in a lack of resulting offline romance; it's disheartening how much digital potential never materializes and time gets lost in the wayside. I tire of marketing both Love Bites and my writing career too; designing flat images for Instagram and interacting with "people" only in this two-dimensional sphere feels far less enjoyable than the actual work done with physically present humans.

I never expected my career to end up as mostly me and a machine, alone.

But I also have an illness I never expected to go chronic either.

Ben and I met in college, getting our fine arts degrees in theater. For much of my life, creative collaboration and conversation have been my passion, my purpose, and, later, my career. I first got diagnosed with Lyme disease when I was twelve, well over a year after illness and misdiagnosis began. Many who get Lyme—an infection of the Borrelia burgdorferi spirochete transferred through the bite of a tick—fully recover. Up to 40 percent of us have symptoms indefinitely.[1] We don't know why. Nor do tests reliably prove if infections in late-diagnosed patients are fully eradicated.[2] In college, test results came back positive again, and I muscled through classes and performances while receiving antibiotic injections and vitamin drips. I thought I was fully recovered, but in my late twenties the bottom dropped out again; I quit my theater and teaching jobs and recovered through nonantibiotic means. In my early thirties, my health started to slip once more. Today, my symptoms fall under the umbrellas of post-treatment Lyme disease syndrome (PTLDS), fibromyalgia, and myalgic encephalomyelitis (ME): specific patterns of nerve, muscle, and joint pain wrapped in overwhelming fatigue.

To thwart complete collapse, I stopped performing and embraced interview, exploring the minds of living humans for print and podcast with the same curiosity I embraced characters for the stage. From the calm of home, I voraciously read books and articles, watch TED Talks, and formulate interview questions, then use my limited energy in dialogue on the phone or in physical presence. This process helps me better understand our world and enjoy my place within it, despite physical limitation.

But in my single-and-sick isolation, I feel too many of my "relationships" now live in gadgets. And I've started to observe that access to instant digital stimulation drives more of us unnecessarily from real-life conversation and into our devices too. This disconnection has started to muddle how I feel about my place in the world—the *joy* I feel in the world itself.

"All this distraction is taking me away from being present," I tell Ben.

On Facebook, the recent horrific Pulse Nightclub shooting has some people I love defending LBGTQ+ rights and other people I love defending gun rights. Debate over the upcoming elections has taken over Twitter, and both Clinton and Trump supporters attack seemingly without remorse. Some humans in my life call other humans words I can't stomach repeating. They curse feminism and scoff at the Black Lives Matter movement.

My brain can't make sense of such derision, such unbound hostility.
I draft missives in response. But then delete them.

That's a lie.

A few times, I've (egotistically) sent out (what I thought was) a smartly crafted set of words. I've expected that, upon reading, the recipient might reflect and come out a kinder, more compassionate person. Instead, they send back something biting and defensive. I'm flummoxed. Embarrassed. Ashamed. Others then chime in with jabs of their own, attacking or defending.

I look at my words again. I ponder them from the opposite perspective.

I consider them as mere symbols on a screen.

Now, I see condescension. Defiance.

I remember: the real and virtual worlds don't always align.

As we curate images and edit words, we craft elevated online versions of ourselves *just a bit better* than we are in three dimensions. As a result, a strong body of research concludes, those of us already feeling low self-esteem particularly reach out to act through these surrogate selves—our avatars, if you will—when needing an ego boost.[3] But, unfortunately, these avatars are devoid of the social cues our brain needs that signal us to "put the brakes on hurting people," as psychologist David DeSteno puts it. I get Professor David on the phone because as researcher, author, and director of Northeastern University's Social Emotions Group, he specializes in maneuvering the emotions I want to better understand. "When you and I are talking face to face, if I'm saying things that are hurtful to you, I see that hurt in your nonverbal expression," he points out. "I can pick up a lot on how you're feeling just by looking at you and seeing your body's response. If I'm not a horrible person, this will tend to make me have some empathy and compassion. Online, you don't see any of that."

Fully fluffed, we're subconsciously primed to see others as less human.

We act more cruelly than we might when someone stands before us.

The same can be said with dating apps. Ben and I talk at length about this confounding Wild West of online etiquette. Just last week I got ghosted. Again. I'd started to feel the age-old heart-thump for a man who was handsome, seemingly intelligent, owned his own small creative business—the good things you learn online—as we moved flirty app correspondence to text, then planned to meet, and then . . . nothing. A few days passed. I checked in with him. Once. Twice. Ghost.

The Internet giveth and the Internet taketh away.

Because the Internet isn't th real.

It shouldn't hurt anymore. But it does.

"I feel helpless in not being able to have a real conversation." I stress to Ben on the show. I've found myself brooding over insults. I play out in my mind hypothetical conversations and relationships that never materialize because I don't *talk* to these people.

I Tweet and erase. I Instagram and erase.

I don't know who I am online anymore!

I'm exhausted from pretending that I do.

I need a break. Even a little one.

"What are you going to do when the impulse comes to check?" Ben asks.

"I have crazy discipline!" I challenge back. "I can do anything for forty days." To help me stay the course, I take all social media and dating apps off of my phone. I remove their pages from my browser history. I set up a social media management program that will let me post articles and updates without my seeing or interacting with feeds. I wonder what thoughts will fill my head when unplugged and alone. Will I read more books? Enjoy lazy walks? How much will I miss online dating? (Or *do* I *hate dating*?)

"Do you have any expectations?" Ben asks as we wrap the segment.

Not expectations, necessarily. But hope.

I can't wander in the fog anymore.

I need to find the path.

And so I have hope that disconnecting might connect me with *it* again.

Or at least show me what *it* is.

INEFFICIENT

June 21. Day One.

I open my eyes and immediately realize how much I need this.

This is how my morning *usually* begins:

Within five minutes of waking, the phone charging two feet from my head is in my hands. First, I open Twitter. Instantly, insecurity skulks: I'm not observationally funny like YA author Jen Doll. ("Memes are the new gluten."[4]) I don't have an emotionally loyal audience like food writer Kat Kinsman or novelist Esmé Weijun Wang. My building jealousy for the spot-on online expression of such lady writers I adore tastes like a morning breath of rotting fish. But I keep scrolling self-flagellatingly until too much "nasty woman" stuff swarms my feed and I switch over to Instagram. But there I see that my pretty pictures haven't gotten as many ♥s as everyone else's pretty pictures. All of a sudden it's like I'm back in high school where my clothes aren't right, and I'm uncomfortable in my skin, and everyone else has their powderpuff pink or NYC punk *so on point* because *their* ♥ count is rollin' in, and so I move over to Facebook, where *actual friends* from high school are deep in digital conversation, and I can't catch up, and now I *really* don't belong and *oh my dog, it's now nine o'clock and where did forty-five minutes of my life go*?!?!

That's every other morning, before this One.

Today, I rise from bed.

I walk Mitra.

I make coffee.

I sit at my desk. I read through press releases announcing menu changes and restaurant openings. I answer invitations, yes and no. I research, write, and send interview questions.

Click, write, archive, delete.

I read my *New York Times* Daily Briefing.[2] Trump faces "the worst financial gap in presidential history," with Clinton's campaign banking thirty-two times his. Florida police defend their delayed actions at the Pulse shooting. The Senate voted down four measures that would curb future gun sales. The trial of Caesar R. Goodson Jr. the police officer charged in the 2015 death of Freddie Gray, the twenty-five-year-old Baltimore man who died of severe spinal injury after being beaten by cops, cuffed, and tossed in the back of a police van is wrapping up. The Senate is blocking President Obama's nomination of Merrick B. Garland to the Supreme Court. I stare at the screen, alone but for my dog and coffee. Shit is tense. It feels like some vengeful Greek god hovers, snarling, with weapons ready. But we can't identify exactly where or on whom its wrath will fall.

I need a social media brain break.

I can't take one.

Ouch.

I dive into more research. Not being able to look on social feeds when prepping interview questions makes this *stupid* cleanse professionally inconvenient. I read a fabulous essay and want to snoop out the writer: *What does she vent on Twitter? What hue is her Instagram palate? I wanna look!* Instead, I schedule a share of her story on *Love Bites'* Twitter feed. (I'm glad I anticipated this. Sharing stories matters.)

By two thirty, I've gotten so much done and my in-box is clear! This never happens but—*dammit*—I can't tweet the victory! Only sixish hours in, triumph mixes with unease.

I catch myself reaching for the phone every. single. time. I rise from my desk. I don't know what to do with myself while the microwave warms my tea. Or when my ancient laptop slowly loads a browser page. Or while I pee.

Am I addicted—like, physically hooked—to social media?

Having been born in the summer of 1981, I fall into a gap between generations X and Y (millennials). We indefinables grew up playing first-generation Nintendo and Oregon Trail. We took classes *to learn how to type.* In high school, dial-up begrudgingly connected us to sketchy AOL chat rooms. In resistance to the staying power of the Internet, my college classmates and I got a professor's plan to have us turn in assignments via e-mail successfully overturned!

Fast forward: I've downloaded and forgotten about too many dating and social network apps to ever want to tally. I navigate basic HTML, own eight URLs, and can edit and upload video, photography, and audio to various platforms (#Freelancer). I've lost count of how much storage I have in the so-not-stable cloud. My college friends plan reunions via Facebook.

How did I get from protest to feeling like I've chopped off a limb?

Have I failed in my use of technology?

Or has the tech presumably designed to make life easier failed me?

"It failed because it got too big," says Amber Case. I reach out to Amber because her expertise touches both technical and personal:

as a user experience tech designer, cofounder and former CEO of the software company Geoloqui, and author of the manual *Calm Technology: Principles and Patterns for Non-Intrusive Design*, Designer-Amber knows how gadgets get made. As a cyborg anthropologist—one who studies the interaction between humans and technology—Anthropologist-Amber questions if they add value to our lives. (Amber prefers cyborg over avatar.)

I ask Amber why it's so hard to moderate use of online media. If I can't stop myself from endless Twitter scrolling or if pop-up videos pull my attention away from the one article I came on a site to read, who is more at fault? Do I blame it or me?

She says we have to first look at such technology as we would any other tool. "Initially, tools empowered us," she explains. "You are shaped by your tools, and you shape your tools. A carpenter, for example, knows the purpose of a hammer. The details of how to use the hammer do not distract from the wood in front of us or the walls we're building. "You're using it to get your job done, and you have your life's work with it," Designer-Amber says. But social media apps are often overcomplicated tools that distract us from our purpose and limit creativity. Our fill in the-blank profiles never look that much different than the next person's. We may think we shape our communities as we use them, but we don't. Instead, designers apply algorithms to prioritize what we see. Ideally, social networks and media companies would be useful tools that connect us in conversation. But Anthropologist-Amber points out these companies are for-profit and publicly traded; we pay them through "a period of time on the web," she explains. They only grow if they attract more of our time. And so they work to keep us clicking.

They're succeeding. Sixty-eight percent of adults in the United States, spanning all generations, are on Facebook now—my poppa was passing my friends digital Jell-O shots before I even had a profile. Three-quarters of users check in daily,[6] and 28 percent of Generation X report being online an average of seven hours a week—more than even millennials. [7]

I sit back and roughly calculate: pre-cleanse me hits that seven-hour mean shortly after my morning coffee. Then there's the constant reaching for the phone every time I rise to walk or pee or because I can't finish a thought . . .

Where did those hours go?

Anthropologist-Amber suggests a test to anyone who asks: "It's super awkward," she jokes. "Go on a news binge on the web. Spend half an hour. Then write down what you remember. Nobody remembers *anything.*"

Day One, I regret so much time lost.

At night, I'm supposed to meet my Soccer-Smart Friend Timmy at a bar to watch Team USA play Argentina in the Copa Americana, but my pain levels are too high for me to venture from home. Instead, I nest in the couch, cranky: I can't hang with Timmy, and now I can't join other Tweeters commenting from isolated pockets either—there is *something* to be said for nerdy-specific online community. But then Timmy starts to text a play-by-play on par with the same expertise I enjoy when we're side-by-side cheering. USA loses 4–0. But I feel particularly thankful for a real friend who virtually sits with me to the last second.

Night One, I drift to sleep with no mindless scrolling to delay me. I can almost feel my fingers again.

ALONELINESS

Sweat prickles at the base of my neck as I walk into the backyard of Roberta's Pizza. It's a sticky Brooklyn summer night; the kind that pushes indefinable black grime into the pores on your face and between the creases of your sandaled toes. But I'm not battling the heat. I've come to a party at Heritage Radio unnervingly alone, testing offline life. I see few other punctual guests and no close friends. I put down my bag and . . .

What do I do now?

Seriously?

What does one *do* in such social situations?

I knew vulnerability would be a factor but—*damn!*—this will take effort.

I immediately regret every decision around what brought me here: I regret the brash intentions broadcasted on this station only two days ago. I regret using up physical energy to trek from Canada to Mexico (Washington Heights to Bushwick). I regret my outfit; a combination of salvaged seventies and hodgepodge Brooklyn designer jewelry that felt artsy in my apartment but now feels juvenile and *wrong*. My skin sticks, and it'd be easier to just grab a cider and a bench and stare into my phone, looking busy until someone I know walks in, *but I can't!*

I take a deep breath.

I pull up my ovaries.

I walk over to a group talking, fortified by the presence of my engineer, David, who immediately asks, "How's the social media cleanse going?" (Huh. I didn't expect it to be a social icebreaker.)

I nervily start recounting the last twenty-four hours, flushing pink; both my university degree in *talking* and on-the-air confidence have evidently left the borough, because I'm awkward. I make a joke about how missing the phone feels like missing a limb . . . and then immediately backtrack because, especially as someone with an illness, I shouldn't so casually joke about bodies. Insecurity now even higher, nothing lands right. As I fumble, I watch where attention goes. David's near my age, but others are full-on millennials. I see phones in hands or pockets . . . but no one reaches to open them? My verbal diarrhea finally fizzles, and others start to voice their online angst. I pop into interview comfort zone—relieved I'm not nearly the only one struggling with this online conundrum—and it's a full fifteen minutes before someone breaks to Google or text.

This feels like a win.

Yes, we're artists at a nonprofit who foster conversation in real time.

And I start to suspect my cleanse invites a "How long can you not . . . ?"

But as we drift for drinks or move to other clusters, I feel less sticky.

In-person conversation should be a little awkward at the start, right? Natural thought doesn't come in ready sound bites or 140-character comebacks. My vulnerability implies I'm not performing an elevated, online version of myself.

I walk up to more people. I get another drink. When I have nothing to say, I listen. When I have no one to talk to, I comb Roberta's vegetable gardens, thrilling at the fragrance and feel of sage and rosemary. (In thirty weeks of shows, I've never noticed them before?) Walking into conversations becomes easier the more I do it.

Donald O. Hebb was a mid-twentieth-century Canadian neuropsychologist. His groundbreaking studies broadened our understanding of synaptic plasticity: the brain's ability to change pending the stimulation we feed it. According to Hebb's Rule, "neurons that fire together, wire together"; when two neurons fire at the same time, their connection strengthens and it becomes easier for them to fire again. Clifford Nass was a communications professor who then proposed that "just as muscles atrophy if they are not continually asked to work, the emotion-processing parts of the brain need to be constantly stimulated by face-to-face interaction to remain effective."[8] If we want to feel more social ease, then we need to feed our malleable brain things like the visual cues Professor David pointed out are vital for empathetic conversation; we need to fire and wire neurons to keep that part of the brain tight.

In my increased isolation, I've fallen out of shape.

Tonight I have fun stretching muscles.

Then a few days pass.

I split time between New York and Connecticut. Back in country mode, I face a weekend watching my Brother Dan and his girlfriend Lizzie's house, alone but for the menagerie of their two cats, my Mitra, and their Georgia the Very Large Wonderdog (henceforth Gigi). Settled on the deck, I sip white wine and take in the suburban bliss. dogs romp merrily in the grass, wind dances salt over from the Long Island Sound, and laughter spills over from neighboring backyards. Purple and red flowers tumble from Lizzie's planters. Bees sing. A sky so blue it's almost saccharine hovers above the trellis over my head. Leafy trees cross my view, revealing puffy clouds beyond. All is color and dimension and definition.

Then it hits.

It's eight thirty on a Friday night.

I have nothing to do and nowhere to be.

All weekend.

Tears fill my eyes.

"We walk!" I rally-cry to the dog-animals.

Down by the shore, relaxed summer revelers stroll. Gigi jumps up onto the stone wall that separates land from sea, Mitra follows suit, and I click photos (and think #WomansBestFriend). The sky shifts to an even more intense hue, bouncing over soft swells. The evening drips tone and temperature perfection. We stride. The dogs yank me in opposite directions, sniffing everything. I smile to every passerby, working both body and brain muscles. I'm thankful for anything that distracts from this increasing . . . pull? . . . at my center; this foreign *thing* that slowly knots and gnaws as we circle back to the house.

I settle again on the porch: wine, feet up, dogs in the yard.

I try to just sit with the scene.

But I can't.

I flip through photos on my phone: dogs by the water, my feet on the table, glass of wine with the sky behind, this luxurious summer paradise. But doing so makes the pull spread. It spreads into a heat. My body *wants* something. It wants something *fierce*. I scan the space, eyes piercing the yard, the sky, searching for this *thing* I can't figure out. Then I see the trellis above my head. I recognize it—the frame of another photo in my phone. I remember.

I spent ten years of my young adult life dating my best friend, Ruark, and we're still friends. Then there was a relationship with a nice guy whose now-wife I chat with on Instagram (just not *right* now). Then a man who broke my heart. Then a delicate haze of a year with a friend who became a lover, then a love, then a lover again, then settled back into a friend.

Between and around them all, others.

And between and around them, solitude.

Then last summer. This porch. And one man.

Together, we walked these dogs down to this water. In this kitchen, he shucked oysters while I made chowder. We filled this table with candles and food and wine. This same sky sank into lavenders and indigoes and then darkness. French music danced delicately from a speaker as we ate slowly, drank good pink wine. Mitra fell asleep on his lap, and mosquitos bit because he suggested we linger. It was the kind of evening that opens to conversation, confession, and trust— the still, quiet, comfortable companionship of early romance. For the first time in a very, very long time, my midthirty-something heart pinged with true possibility.

It didn't work out.

I lift my gaze up to the sky, now too bright and blinding.

The pull in my stomach tightens; another starts in my throat.

The absence, so palpable.

I have no one to experience my life with.

There is no one here. No one checking in.

And now no way to share this with digital friends who can then . . .

What?

I am isolated, alone, and petrified.

My chest starts closing in.

What is happening to me?

No answer.

Distract! Distract!

I race inside, bring my laptop back to the porch, and start streaming a video of a steam train barreling through the Scottish Highlands. As the train cuts through the still, expansive lochs, I force my senses into sharp alert. *Eyes, focus!* I roll wine around on my tongue. *Taste!* I concentrate on the rhythm of the movement down tracks. *Listen!* I feel my breath slow as it slices through moors and mountains.

I'm captivated.

I'm worried.

When did I become such a cliché?

At thirty-four, I have aged into a group of socially suspicious single women expected to both proudly defend our uncoupled status and hide any vulnerabilities surrounding it. It doesn't matter that I've never foamed at the mouth for a white dress or picket fence. Or how often I professionally profess that not everyone wants a partner, how there are more noble life ambitions to meet, or how women can have as much (safe, consensual) sex as we want. Tonight, I find myself the star of the quintessential rom-com opening montage: a woman drinking wine, alone, panic-attack unlovable, not understanding how I got here, or why I deserve it.

I force my attention back to the train.

I remind myself that relationships can be whatever we want them to be.

My friends Lyndsey and Christian live in Virginia; my friends Rose and Rex in California. I know Lyndsey from college; Rose from childhood. We've worked to not let distance, career, hardship, or time fray our friendships. I watched their romances blossom and then partook in their weddings with genuine joy. Their unions could have pulled at our intimacy, but instead, Christian one day affectionately called me his second "wifey." Independent of this, Rex later claimed me as the same for him and Rose. These gestures of masculine affection speak highly of their relationship security, our long-term female friendships, and how they gently recognize my need to give and receive love. We support one another like true partners: they judge my gentleman callers; I referee their squabbles. We regularly dissect our respective jobs, homes, and health. We travel together. We plan how we'll move through the world as humans with no children and the struggles of aging adulthood. We share triumphs, milestones, and new experiences. Like Lyndsey and Christian's trip to Scotland in a few weeks; that's why I'm watching the video. As the train continues to wind and wander, my brain ponders the silly mystery of life that wound me from a decade of coupledom into and around and out of love time and again, to here, where I sit alone but for the unspoken presence of two wives and two husbands whom I love fiercely.

And who, I trust, love me.

I feel the panic in my body ease.

Sherry Turkle is a renowned social psychologist and MIT professor. Over decades of studying the effect of technology on humans, she has observed that our constant digital connection gives us simulated feelings of connectedness—we *think* we are never alone and, therefore, can never feel lonely. "But we are at risk because it is actually the reverse: if we are unable to be alone, we will be more lonely," she says in her book *Reclaiming Conversation: The Power of Talk in a Digital Age.*[9] Turkle calls the kind of unplugged solitude I've forced upon myself a "state of conscious retreat, a gathering of the self." If we better understand ourselves during solitude, then we better know who we are overall. We can better see others for who they are too. And what parts we best play in each other's lives. "The capacity for solitude makes relationships with others more authentic," she promises.

I could call my wives right now. I know they would listen and soothe my sadness, as they have many times before. I think of others—Ben, my mother, my father, my siblings, my nana and poppa—who would answer too. I could use my phone as a *phone*, a tool even Anthropologist-Amber can praise.

But I don't need to call anyone now.

With my entire being, I trust I do not lack for love tonight.

This stops the craving for an online fix.

And pining for a hypothetical future fifth, final spouse.

I watch the video fade into darkness, the sound of the train with it. I look up at the night sky, at its indigo hush inside the familiar frame. And I glow.

UNTETHERED

"I'm someone a little different on the road, and that vacation from my home self feels like a great sleep after a long day."[10]

So begins Kristin Newman in her memoir, *What I Was Doing While You Were Breeding*. A Los Angeles TV writer, Kristin also spent her twenties coupled. In her thirties, she made up for lost single time traversing the globe: climbing faraway snowy mountains, bedding exotic men, and sleeping under glaciers. "You don't know that you have a Spidey sense 'till you go out and do it and have a good experience," she tells Ben and me years later on *Love Bites*. "It's so empowering. It completely changed how I felt about myself in my early thirties."

Back in 2009, Ruark and I were about to (amicably) break up. I would soon move to Ohio for a new job, giving us some distance to start over. Shit was both exciting and intense. To clear my head, I borrowed money, packed cameras, and flew to London to stay with a friend. Then I crossed on a ferry to Ireland and bussed from Dublin to Knock to Cork and back to Dublin, finding my center again (but there officially to interview street performers I hoped to turn into a documentary). For that trip, I got my very first smartphone—an Android. It was a blessed safety net I used to hastily pay a due credit card bill or to plead with the bus company after I got dropped off on a grassy knoll halfway between Dublin and Knock and the driver chugged off with my suitcase still in the undercarriage!! (Irish bus lady: "We'll have it back in your hands before your transfer bus comes through. Go into the pub and have a pint." They did. I did. *Erin go bragh*.)

Seven years later, I'm hacking my way out of a strangling smartphone net.

I'd gone into this cleanse knowing two short trips lay ahead.

I want to face them with Solo-Seeker Kristin's sense of adventure.

I want back the phone-free thrill I remember of yesteryears

But I can't get the damned phone outta my field of vision.

First, I'm driving to Newport, Rhode Island, to meet Mom and Big Sis Jessica for a few days, a trek I've done every summer for as long as I can remember. The highway stretches out inky black. Just me and my Lil' Blue Subaru for a few hours, my attention repeatedly pulls to the three-by-five rectangle mounted on my dash. The navigation app is open, but the path ahead clear, it lazily moves in time with my wheel. My fingers itch to touch it and . . . what?

In *Calm Technology*, Designer-Amber explains primary, secondary, and tertiary attention, using automobiles as an example [11] "Primary attention is visual and direct," she details. Maneuvering three-thousand-pound Lil' Blue demands that my eyes stay focused on the road, the other cars around us, and the lights and signs directing our way; these make driving a "primary task" and top priority. Then my peripheral senses need to scan windows, check mirrors, and gauge pedals, requiring "secondary attention" and making driving also a "secondary task." Finally, analyzing the texture of radio knobs and glancing at dashboard warning lights make driving require "tertiary attention" and therefore also a "tertiary task." Altogether, cars are designed by such attention and task priority. Like Amber's example of the hammer and the wall, the tool is designed so that we can use it simply and safely.

Smartphones—with their small size, touch screens, and a primary purpose that is *not controlling a death bomb on wheels*—also require primary attention. They have no place in our hands while we're also behind a wheel. Too many of us use them despite laws and our good sense guiding us otherwise, and thousands of people die monthly as a result.[12]

As hours pass, I'm disgusted by how often my gaze flies toward the phone. I'm sickened. Ashamed.

Thankful for the reset.

Finally off the highway, I meander breezy Rhode Island backroads. With each familiar turn, anticipation builds. I roll down the windows to a rush of honeysuckle and jasmine. I glide over the Jamestown bridge and take in big gulps of salty air—it's a sparkling, stunning day. Over the Newport Bridge, I cry at what look like diamonds bouncing off water. I vow to make the most of this untethered time with the women I love and jump, exhausted from the short ride, into their arms. Over the next few days we slam trays of shellfish and drink martinis until we giggle. (I can't Instagram the spread but don't give a damn.) We sit outside, waiting for an architectural tour, and I notice how Japanese maples cast a golden-red glow against wood shingles, the humid air lending texture to the light as it dances off stained glass. Inside, I discover patterns of limbs and leaves etched into dark wood.

There is always something new to see.

I'm learning how to look again.

I take a book to the White Horse Tavern (the oldest bar in the US!), planning to kill an hour with a pint and a book, but instead end up entranced by John the bartender's monologue about colonial history, pirate hangings, and Revolutionary currency. Alone at another bar, watching Portugal play in the Eurocup, I get chatted up by a young boat builder who gives me recommendations for places to see in

Barcelona, where I'll be in two weeks. My attention is not sucked into a phone. My face is alert and my body language inviting. Humans are marvelous—I'd almost forgotten!—and I wonder how many people I *haven't* met because I was distracted by the gadget in my hand.

Before I head home, Mom and I drive to our favorite rocky cliff. We stare out at the expanse. The water is rough, and the summer wind whips. I taste salt I cannot see. I *feel* things stirring. "It's a chance to not think about anything else," a nearby fisherwoman, Corey Wheeler Forrest, describes to me of the pull of her sea. "It's like meditating." My gaze blurs on the horizon. I breathe it all in and out. As the salt, wind, and waves swirl, I ask the ocean to carry away the stuffy, crunchy parts within me.

I hear Solo-Seeker Kristin:

"Get on a plane by yourself and go have an adventure.

And so, a few weeks later, I fly to Barcelona for the weekend.

Readying in New York, I spin this in my head as a luxurious glam getaway: I'm being flown first class, put up in a swanky hotel, dined out at high-end restaurants, given spa services, and guided through Gaudi's greatest hits, all paid for by companies who want me to write about them. I'm beyond broke and turning thirty-five, so I figure there's no better way to solo celebrate than "leap and have adventures" à la SS-Kristin!

But by the time I land in Barcelona, I am anything but glam. I probably shouldn't have attempted this to begin with, given my middling health; I navigate the flight with pain levels well above thirty-five thousand feet. Then the sponsoring European airline has me fly *past* Spain for a layover, so the trip takes about twenty hours total. Stepping into the hot Catalonian sun, I immediately meet a sleek driver and team of black-clad concierges and well-heeled fellow guests (who can afford the place), looking like a crumpled pajama.

I breathe.

I've done press trips before.

I've written hundreds of stories—that's why they want me here.

I plaster on a smile and jump into journalist mode.

I've got this.

Famous last words.

I scramble to navigate three languages and a messy itinerary: Do I need a cab? No, *this time* there's a car waiting. I'm taking an unexpected interview? I'm taking an unexpected interview! I frantically scribble notes and make up questions on the fly. I drink too much coffee (because, writer) and drink too much wine (because, Spain). Finally, in bed, jet lag keeping sleep at a tease, I FaceTime First Wife Lyndsey, crying from overexhaustion.

People are friendly. New cities are exciting.

But everything is new. Time is tight.

My body burns. It screams: *Why did you do this to us . . . ?*

And yet . . .

Alone at a corner table in a downtown restaurant, I notice the loneliness that floored me only a few weeks ago has opened to curious observation. I enjoy every bite of *tortilla*, every sliver of *jamón*. I sink into a hot tub at the spa, gaze through a window across endless sea, and thrill at feeling so far from home, alone. At the hotel's patio restaurant, I talk with the chef, take notes in my Moleskin, and then just . . . sit. My eyes appreciate the fading light. My ears take in muffled conversations. My body settles into the warm Spanish night. I take it all in: the details of the food, the people, the warm breeze on my bare arms.

"When we let our minds wander, we set our brains free," No-Tech Turkle says.

If able to share this oh-so-Instagrammable excursion, I'd be snapping, editing, and uploading every course—the expectations of every food writer abroad. I'd tag the restaurants, the hotel, the tour guides, and the magazines that will publish these stories. I'd track likes and reposts.

I'd miss all this.

Has my creativity suffered from a pressure to market?

When did I start considering myself a "brand"?

How did I fall so willingly into this habit?

"Norms and anthropology," Anthropologist Amber says without hesitation. "It's anything that's the norm where everybody thinks, *this is the exact same way it's always been.*" She compares it to the proverbial frog in a pot of water, not realizing it has slowly come to a boil. Online, we see successful people in the elevated cosmos we've created. We think (or are told) we, too, are nothing without a "platform." Eventually, wired neurons progressively have us assuming *this is the way.*

Tonight, I jump from the pot.

I tweet-and-erase and Instagram-and-erase because I don't know who I am online anymore. Well, maybe I don't know who I am offline anymore either. But I choose to not be a *brand.* When this cleanse is over, I'll figure out how I can retain an online presence—one honest to the messy, creative, risk-taking, fail-making, conversation-bumbling human I am.

For now, I'm living in real time.

My second and final full day in Barcelona, I steal a few unscheduled hours between appointments and navigate narrow streets until I find the Plaça del Sol; the Newport boat builder's recommendation for a social, lively scene. But I've come early on a Monday morning. Closed apartment windows flank the empty open square. Only a few locals shuffle to the underground parking garage. If there was a Catalonia equivalent to tumbleweeds, now's about when one would whirl by. I've been racing for weeks now. I could use some unexpected emptiness.

I sit at a café, just to have somewhere to sit.

I sip coffee I don't need. I order food I can't eat.

I page through a book I don't feel like reading.

I look at nothing in particular.

I'm entirely off the clock. Nothing to do, nowhere to be.

I feel the familiar knot of panic.

I've been too busy to ask myself much these last few weeks, using work and travel and life as an excuse. This unplugged solitude—this second "gathering of the self"—leaves me with a new question that twists me up inside:

What am I doing here?

I flew for a day to be in a foreign city for two? I can barely decipher my mess of notes and probably won't land further stories from the extra interviews, so this won't be a financially lucrative trip. If being honest, I probably could have written the stories from my desk back at home. Do I make irresponsible work decisions? Is this why my career has stalled and I'm so broke?

What am I actually even doing here?!

Turning thirty-five in another country had seemed like a mini-Solo-Seeker-Kristin adventure, but here I am: bored! Killing time at a café that might as well be back in Washington Heights for all I'm appreciating it, having a mid-midlife crisis in discovering that I *don't know who the hell I am*!

No-Tech Turkle points out we rely on our phones to escape boredom and anxiety. But that "boredom and anxiety are signs to attend more closely to things, not to turn away."[13]

Without a phone, I have no choice but to attend the scene around me.

A woman at the next table feeds her tiny dog. A friend with a toddler joins. The little girl throws a ball across the *plaça*. Over and over they play. The friends talk.

I attend to the scene inside of me. Maybe it's okay to be bored and frustrated with my life while also in Barcelona? Maybe it's enough to ask questions and accept that I don't have answers for them just yet?

The happy child and dog run out of the shadows and back into the sun.

I leave coins and uneaten food on the table and start walking.

I pass residential areas and cafes. I casually peruse shops. I get a little lost, but the Spidey sense Kristin referred to kicks in and the sea pulls me in the general direction I need to head, so I don't worry I lazily meander, running my fingers along ancient stone walls. The sun is strong. Hours pass, and I start to ache. I sink, exhausted, on to the steps of the Basilica of Santa Maria del Mar. The sensation reminds me of doing the same on the steps of Saint Paul's after wandering London equally untethered so many years ago. And then after I got my suitcase back from the bus in Ireland, when I made it to Knock and spent two days praying in their humble shrine.

I look around and recognize no faces.

I stand, smile, and shake off the final bits of a net that no longer traps me.

UNGROUNDED

Night falls on Day Forty.

I'm not foaming at the mouth . . . but I am curious.

I check Facebook. Then Twitter. Then Instagram.

It's *un*fulfilling.

I missed a college friend's visit because my classmates used

Facebook to coordinate reunion plans. (Oh, the irony.) I lost a few followers, but I gained some too. No editor voiced concern about a drop in my readership. I take passive delight in birthday messages from a few days prior. Then I put the phone down.

"The Greeks had these concepts of *kairos* and *chronos* time," Anthropologist-Amber tells me. "*Kairos* being where you lose time. You forget about it, you watch a sunset, you fall in love. And then *chronos* as the always on, industrial time. With technology, we kind of slip into a bad *kairos*." By my unplugged birthday, I'd traded the new model for classic *kairos* again.

I turned thirty-five in Barcelona, digging my toes in the sand and watching the sun rise over the beach. Hours later, confidently meandering the airport in Norway during a delayed layover, I casually chatted with travelers from around the world, sipped bad airport wine, and fell lost in a book. Finally, my face pressed to the plane's window, mesmerized, I savored every second of the raging downpour that brought a double rainbow out from the clouds just as we barreled through mist and climbed up into the air.

That very long day remains locked tight in my mind's eye.

My heart warms every time I think back on it.

In her TED Talk, Anthropologist-Amber uses the phrase "panic architecture" to describe how our tech-laden society constantly shoves information at us to the point that we can never keep up. Without time to think, digest, or choose, we are structured for constant overwhelm. "When you get dissipated, where is the time to remember? Where is the reflective time *not* shared?" she then asks me.

Day Forty, I sit with phone in hand, understanding how there was no way I could identify my fog until I disassembled some of this panic architecture, until I jumped from the boiling pot and strengthened some brain muscles. I can now somewhat see a path . . . I just don't yet know where it leads. I sense there's more to this story than one forty-day cleanse, more accidental addictions to uncover and habits to break.

I think I want to keep going?

Yes. I want to keep going.

For how long can I push my "crazy discipline"?

Six months?

A year!

Yes. I'll call it . . .

~~My Year of Abstinence~~.

My Year, Without.

~~MY YEAR OF ABSTINENCE~~

THE ME, WITHOUT

We all have a fascinating gooey cluster of subcortical nuclei nestled by our brainstem called the basal ganglia. Responsible for base motor control, this fascinating nub stores the stuff we learned in early childhood, like the repetitive motions that taught us to crawl or wave. They also trigger social cues, like thanking someone immediately after they pass the peas.

Basically, the basal ganglia store habits.

Studies begun in the 1990s by members of MIT's McGovern Institute for Brain Research have mapped the brains of rats as they learned how to navigate mazes. The rats would hear a "click," a door would open, and the rats would start sniffing and exploring, neurons firing and wiring as they meandered walls and pathways. Eventually, the rats found a reward of chocolate or sugar water at the end, which released a happy rush of the neurotransmitter dopamine into their brains. Learning the route, their basal ganglia would store the sensory clues. As they repeated the pattern—click, wander, find

29

happy reward—the rats subsequently navigated faster. The parts of the brain taking in the sensory stimulation simmered down, and the basal ganglia took over. The rats had learned to move by habit.[14]

The MIT researchers thus established the *habit loop*: cue, routine, reward.

"The brain has an absolutely fabulous system for getting reward signals," commented lead neuroscientist Ann M. Graybiel in an MIT interview.[15] She notes this system is so smart yet sensitive that we're completely unaware it's happening. Such habits take a long time to build and we often craft them unintentionally, not recognizing cues or even subtle rewards.

With this new knowledge, my confused inner monologue these last forty days makes more sense.

In his book *The Power of Habit*, investigative reporter Charles Duhigg points out that the active decision-making parts of the brain turn off during the routine part of the loop, and so "unless you deliberately fight a habit—unless you find new routines—the pattern will unfold automatically."[16] To successfully attack bad habits, we often identify the cue and replace the routine with a healthier option that leads to a similar or better reward. Instead of eating too much chocolate cake at the end of a rough day, we go to a book club or a yoga class and feel renewed pride and determination.

Anthropologist-Amber considers online media a *non*calm tech tool that delivers a dopamine-rushing reward. I'd identified a routine cued up pretty much by any quick real-life distraction. In these last forty days, I successfully broke myself of the habit. But habit loops run on a *really* tight cue-*routine*-reward trio. Because I didn't replace the routine, I had to wrestle my brain like a whining, writhing muscle monkey, left with no choice but to face wherever the present environment and my panicked thoughts took me.

It was scary. And exciting.

I want more.

I wonder: can it be this simple? Can abstaining from routine be more effective than all of the self-help programs I've tried of yore?

The URL www.MyYearOfAbstinence.com is available. It's cheeky. I like it. I buy it and set up a blog. But people assume I'm giving up sex for a year. (Ha! *Nope.*) I change the title of my self-self-help project to *My Year, Without* and set ground rules.

1. I WILL REMOVE ONE HABIT AT A TIME: Like a pebble tossed in a pond, I want to see how far ripples spread from one habit to other areas of my life. I can't do that if I'm dropping rocks everywhere.

2. I WILL REMOVE ONLY HABITS I GENUINELY WANT TO CHALLENGE: My self-control is only effective if I have skin in the game. Before each "Challenge," I'll ponder what in my life might not be serving me well. If I confidently conclude its absence will significantly alter my playing field, I'll go without it.

3. I'LL CHOOSE THE LENGTH OF EACH CHALLENGE AS FEELS APPROPRIATE: I find no scholarly agreement that it takes twenty-one or two hundred days to break a habit anyway.

4. CHALLENGES CAN'T INVOLVE SPENDING MONEY: I don't have money to spend. But also, as I'm focusing on shifting my inner life, paying for a fancy spa retreat doesn't seem above board here.

5. CHALLENGES SHOULD INSPIRE A GREATER "WHY?": I am thirsty for change. But I'm more curious

about the me within the greater picture. I'll look
to anyone who can help me understand where my
journey fits in our collective whole.

6. I'LL JOURNAL CHANGES: I'll use changes in my
    physical health, social interactions, and sense of
    self as meters. Going offline gave me space to pay
    attention. Paying attention makes a difference.

Where am I at the start of my official Year?

I'm sick . . . But I don't aim to cure my illness.

I'm single ... But I don't expect to manifest happily ever after.

I'm broke . . . But I don't want money to be my due north ever.

Where does this leave me, *without*?

CHAPTER CHALLENGE 2

NO SHOPPING

CHALLENGE: No Shopping (nonessential items)

TIME LINE: Ninety days

RULES: I will not buy any nonessential item, including clothes, shoes, home goods, office supplies, books, toiletries, superfluous foods (upscale items, treats, etc.), or on-the-go coffees.

ADDENDUM: If I *need* a jolt of caffeine, etc., I can buy it. If I use up every single lip balm or all the shampoos in my shower, I can restock *one*. I will assess want from need—and choice from habit—with honesty.

INDEBTED

Satisfaction is subjective.

In the 1980s, psychologist Ed Diener penned the term "subjective well-being" as a measure of varied happiness among individuals. Rather than quantifying by income, health, or production output, Diener's pioneering studies showed how measurements of subjective well-being might better predict the overall health of a society; I might get a similar rush of satisfaction tracking down the one cricket in my neighborhood as you do launching a work project, watching your child sing in a school concert, or hiking the Himalayas. Our income, health, and production output might vary wildly, but we could, theoretically, be equally happy. In turn, the societies in which we live could prove equally robust.

I struggle with income, health, and production output.

I want to cultivate my well-being.

It seems the subjective part is a good place to start.

But, first, I have to face some practicalities.

I question wealth: Can money buy me love? Or is money the root of all evil today? Because Dr. Happiness Diener's studies show money *does* buy some measure of happiness, though only to a point. There's a threshold. If we can afford essential securities of clean air, water, shelter, food, clothing, health care, etc., then we're pretty much as happy as rich-and-classy Colin Firth (#MrDarcyForever). Diener points out that great wealth often comes with sacrifice of the things that bring us subjective well-being: lost time with family or friends, the sacrifice of hobbies, etc. Additionally, we acclimate to whatever material goods we have; I probably love Lil' Blue as much as Colin loves his Aston Martin (not that I know for *sure* he drives an Aston Martin or anything). Income isn't a significant factor in the happiness of the person who makes five million dollars more than the person who makes fifty thousand. As long as needs of safety are met, wealth plays little difference in subjective well-being.[17]

But at the start of my official Year, I struggle to pay for basic securities.

I take full responsibility for my current financial conundrum, but I inherited a storied emotional relationship with money. My father emigrated in the 1960s with his family from the Azores islands of Portugal, speaking no English; my mother grew up in blue-collar Bridgeport, Connecticut. Extremely hard work brought their success, and they spent abundantly to show our uppity white-collar Connecticut town that our family was as good as anyone else. My parents were (and are) ceaselessly generous. We often had cousins, grandparents, friends-of-friends, or, once, an entire family living with us for months on end. Twice-yearly parties welcomed a hundred guests at a time: in the summer, we tapped kegs and steamed lobsters over an open fire; New Year's Eve started with a buffet dinner and DJ'd dancing, and ended with Dad frying shrimp at 3:00 a.m. before friends passed out all over the house. I pity the people who live in our home after us; for years to come, they'll have our friends walking in through doors they always assume open to them, yelling, "Hey, Raposos!"

In me, such generous spending habits blended with an equally unstoppable work ethic and the "shoot for the stars" trope typical of such wealthy suburban communities of the booming late 1990s. In adulthood, my busy hands bartended, nannied, taught, catered, cooked, and did whatever else needed to make a buck while I built a creative career. I made little and so couldn't save. But I trusted my ability to work and preferred community over economy. Then illness resurfaced and cycled, my inability to generate income compounding with medical bills. I've shifted my career and lifestyle to better ride the tide and I publish stories constantly, but the tag of "middling successful writer" doesn't seamlessly equate to paying down the bills. And so I have of late lived in denial about how starkly I need to face reality:

I am thirty-five years old and over twelve grand in credit card debt.

I spend more than I save, and I can't physically work more to catch up.

It's time for a Challenge that will stare down my spending.

But where does my money even go?

My closet of fast fashion, thrift buys, and inherited duds assumes I never stopped teaching art to kindergarteners in the 1970s. My room looks like a farming hipster grannie dropped out of design school second semester. My glass computer desk came from Staples, my vintage steamer trunk masterfully restored by Poppa. I stole shelves Dad made from four-by-fours, painted them blue, and now cookbooks live on them. Sure, I aspire to look my age and curate a style. But I'm sorta fine with this mélange.

So where does my money go?!

I print a profit and loss statement for the last few months because I'm an adult. (And then drip tea all over them because I'm a hot mess.)

I see times when I've unnecessarily picked up the tab. Maybe I spend too much on car insurance? My pharmacy receipts are certainly higher than the costs of the prescriptions I purchase there. The amount I spend in clients' restaurants leaves room for improvement. My grocery bills are hefty . . .

I'm sure I can trim. I just don't see where.

If money only guarantees happiness when paying for securities, then I will only buy those. For ninety days, I'll not buy any nonessential *anything*. I'll replace only what I use up and observe changes in my body, bank account, social interactions, and the way I feel on the sidewalk or in a store with a little less *stuff* on and around me.

I'll remove *excess*. I hope to discover *essential*.

THE **RIGHT** STUFF

I love my Second Wife Rose and Second Husband Rex to the point that I made the three-tiered cake for their wedding on the small Caribbean island of Saint Croix out of the miniature oven in my hotel room. To do so, I squeezed my KitchenAid standing mixer into a carry-on suitcase and lugged it from JFK to Puerto Rico to Saint Croix. But not only the mixer. I also Tetris'd cardboard cake rounds, serrated pastry knives, long wooden dowels, bottles of vanilla extract, two aprons, towels, and various baking odds and ends. A bathing suit, dress, and kitten heels went into the duffel on my shoulder. That cake was a glorious adventure.

Today, an equally enigmatic puzzle of a laundry bag *tortures my soul!*

I'm schlepping to Bro Dan and Lizzie's for a week, and their delicate-cycle Kenmore calls to my silky whites like a siren. Into a what's more mesh than bag, I'm shoving leggings, nightgowns, sheets, dog blankets, and crumpled skirts wherever I can squish an inch, until it bursts and spews the lot all over the floor. One of three wire rods making the frame splits from the base. Red in the face, I gingerly ninja-balance it together when—*shit-pop-dammit!*—a second rod cracks. I junk the frame to the side, resigned, and take in the chaos.

Day Four of this Challenge.

A new laundry bag feels like an *essential* purchase.

I load Amazon, start browsing . . . and stop.

"*Essential* means food, shelter, health care . . . ," I remind myself.

I tie small knots in the mesh.

What laundry I can't Jenga into it goes into a duffel.

The bag burns my fingers from apartment, to car, to house.

This *without* doesn't feel like a win.

I'm not sure what I'm to learn from the struggle.

Four days later, blisteringly hot, I've scrambled from Connecticut to Brooklyn for *Love Bites* via train and subway. Now, Ben and I head back to Manhattan, where I'll catch a train at Grand Central Station and puff straight back to the burbs. As we dissect the episode, I roll a fresh-squeezed strawberry lemonade around my mouth so sensually I'm almost embarrassed. I let Ben take a few sips and revel in relaxed satisfaction for a long day, until his face shifts:

"Wait, aren't you cheating with the lemonade?!?"

Argh! Only a block from Heritage Radio, all it had taken was a chalkboard sign scribbling out—*We Have Fresh-Squeezed Strawberry Lemonade!*—and my wallet responded—*yes!*—before any other part of my brain had a say in the matter. I had bought without thought.

Am I a boringly stereotypical *cue-routine-reward* rat?

Did a chalkboard invitation become a habit loop cue?

When finishing art school, Roko Belic asked one of his professors what he should consider for a job: "If you want to make money, go into advertising," the professor had said. "That's what ninety-five percent of you guys are going to do." Had Roko listened, he might have inadvertently sold me Lil' Blue, or one of the shirts in my closet I rarely wear. Instead, Roko became a filmmaker. His joyous documentary, *Happy*, explores where topics like family, wealth, health, nature, community, and work collide with the psychology of happiness.

"I remember the first time I cried in a movie," he shares with me. "I was an early teenager, and I saw *The Color Purple* with my mom. I had never cried in front of my mom because of an emotional experience. I had cried a million times for skinning my knee or breaking my leg, but never for that sense of deep love or empathy. So as the lights came up, I was trying to hide my tears. Think about the filmmakers who made that film, and the writers, and the actors. Most of the people with those skills are making TV commercials. If the most talented artists—people who deal with emotions, convey ideas, process life experience, and reflect that back to society—are convincing us to buy shit we don't need, of course there's going to be a problem in our societal psyche!"

I first hear the phrase "hedonic treadmill" in *Happy*, when Roko interviews psychologist Tim Kasser. In his book *The High Price of Materialism*, Kasser dissects decades of empirical data to connect our materialistic desires with feelings of unhappiness and insecurity. He first explains how and why the "extrinsic" desires we *think* will make us happy—the "right" house, clothes, electronics, car, makeup, etc.— actually don't. Our bodies do "require some material comforts to survive," Kasser agrees with Dr. Happiness Diener, citing a feeling of safety and security as an emotional reason for this. But across cultures, income ranges, ages, and genders, once those needs are met, "a strong focus on materialistic values is often a symptom or manifestation of a personal history characterized by a relative failure in need satisfaction," he outlines.[18] Without realizing it, we're often seeking unfulfilled "intrinsic" emotional or psychological needs—things like self-esteem, connection with others, and pride in ourselves—when we reach for material goods. This is how companies who hire talented artists snare us through advertising: they promise *that car* will make us feel successful or *those clothes* beautiful and admired. Magazine covers and billboards promise that happiness is only one fancy perfume, snazzy headphone, or backyard patio scene away.

But once we have the pretty picture and are still not happy?

There's the promise of something even better ahead.

Hence, a hedonic treadmill.

I bought Lil' Blue for its affordability, comfort, and rugged durability. Years later, I don't aspire to Colin's Aston Martin; I don't think of myself as focused on extrinsic goals. But I do cry at every single Subaru commercial—"Love. It's what makes a Subaru a Subaru."—and a flowery chalkboard sign on a steamy Brooklyn sidewalk was enough to cue me into buying lemonade.

Habit loop + hedonic treadmill + artists making advertisements = I buy short-term satisfaction without thought? Is *that* where my money goes?

Back in Connecticut, I face my weakest weakness head-on. "Books have the same irresistible temptation for me that liquor has for its devotee," my kindred spirit L. M. Montgomery once said (to someone else). "I cannot withstand them." I agree. On the first day of this Challenge, I'd found myself in The Strand bookstore with Second Wife Rose. SW has excellent taste in literature. I find myself tearing through her recommendations, screaming because *why does no one deliver tacos at 3:00 a.m. when I'm famished and there are chapters that beg finishing*?! We hadn't planned a stop in Bibliophile Wonka Land on the first day of my withdrawal period, but there we were: she collecting and I, empty-handed, adding names to my Goodreads list while she pointed and summarized for my future cache.

Later, I tallied the titles I would have bought if unreined.

I'd saved eighty bucks.

Still, I won't last three months without books.

I joke that my hometown is uppity. But it's practically Stars Hollow for all its bucolic Connecticut charm—especially the public library. I enter its cool, hushed halls and, within minutes, a blessed librarian revives my sleeping account. I browse tall shelves, sniffing spines and rubbing fingers on bindings, my fix restored. Recommendations call from every aisle end, and I'm almost panic-stricken by choice overwhelm until I remember: I can come back for more! As often as I want! A Michael Chabon novel and collection of James Joyce come with me.

In a few weeks, I'm headed to the Azores with Dad and my *tios* (uncles) and packing light and so, thinking ahead, I use my restored library card on the digital platform too: I download the OverDrive App, which syncs with my library's catalog, which pushes loans to Amazon, which transfers them on to my iPad via a free Kindle app. I execute this albeit messy system in only thirty minutes and download three books, feeling like Hermione Granger with a wand. From a tiny island in the middle of the Atlantic, I'll be able to return them and get more. Magic machines, indeed.

But then I wonder: in an age of Amazon, cheap books, and digital sharing, how are libraries staying alive?

"Experiences!" enthuses Lindsey Rupp. Lindsey's a retail reporter for Bloomberg and the cohost of their (fabulously fun) *Material World* podcast. I ask her how my spending reduction fits in with current trends among my demographic. "In general, consumers your age are moving toward buying less stuff," she tells me. "Consumers want to spend their money on experiences, on something that's authentic, or on something that has meaning." Without prompting, she pulls this back to social media, pointing out that a photo in front of a waterfall gets more ♥s than a new sweater. Libraries staying relevant in the one-click age offer events and create a welcoming space to linger. Indeed, in the rush of my revived fix, I find myself returning to the Stars Hollow library when I don't need a book, typing in the courtyard under the shade of a tree or nestling at a workstation. When stir-crazy at my New York desk, the public library's dramatic Rose Room offers heavy wooden chairs, massive windows, a Beaux Arts painted ceiling, and security guards guiding tourists away—I am among hundreds of heads bent over work or study, breathing and focused, together. Mom and I become members of the nearby Morgan Library & Museum, too, calmly wandering exhibits and partaking in events. I eagerly await the

Stars Hollow book sale, when I can buy again. I mark author readings, classes, and film screenings at all three.

Incidentally, my library pics get a decent amount of love on IG. But that's not the point. Going without new books helps me rediscover a community I didn't realize I was missing: fellow book nerds, writers outside the food world, and characters within the books themselves. And as I flip pages in my cozy corner armchair, I better value the shared materials in my hands.

This makes me question books easefully bought with a click now lining the shelves around me, unread. Digital books linger on my iPad too. "We consider somebody that hoards newspapers or cats to be mentally disturbed," Anthropologist-Amber points out. "But now we hoard pictures of cats and news articles on our computers, and because they don't take up any weight, we don't notice them. We don't notice because it's 'normal,' all these unhealthy habits we have."

Are my hoarded, unread books an unhealthy waste of money and energy?

I start to feel sick as I look around and witness all the items I spend no time appreciating or loving. Taking responsibility, I start to analyze. I accept (after a touch of shame) that there are some titles I'll never read; I put them in a bin to donate to my library community. I make shelves of must-read priorities; I can now see a clear to-do list. Finally, I put my worn hardcovers in prime spots, arranging favorite pieces of pottery and treasures around them.

The books look happier! Healthier! Special!

I sit in my corner chair, admiring them.

Then I broaden my gaze.

I don't own significant excess. But I also don't use all I own.

I see *just a little too much* everywhere.

At my vanity, everything is sparkly and pretty . . . but if I have to actively remind myself to use a highlighter pencil or liquid eyeliner twice a year? With a deep breath, I start sorting. I own dozens of lip colors but only use two subtle shades of Burt's Bees Tinted Lip Balm to the point that I've worn them out and gotten to rebuy them during this Challenge; I thin down those I accept I definitely *don't* like. I see a blusher I've had for a decade, aging eyeshadow that doesn't vary much from one palate to another, samples from subscriptions I've never used ... I clear out, recycling older items and setting aside others for friends.

Again—more space. Special stuff.

I next stank-eye the clothes in my closet and bins under the bed. I've often wanted to do one of those supersatisfying purges people talk about when Marie Kondo-ing or undergoing a breakup makeover. But in my adult life, I've never had enough disposable income to enjoy shopping to the point that I can buy satisfying clothes in excess.

I do see one area I need to address though.

My weight fluctuates with my illness, and so over the years I have progressively saved clothes in various sizes, anticipating future needs. I'm now at the high end of my weight. I don't feel right in my skin. Infuriatingly, I can't work out to work it off. This irks me daily. But pulling tiny clothes several sizes down from the lot, I set a goal to never be *too thin* because of illness again—the clothes in my hand are not the right me either. Into bags, I mercilessly shove all clothing from my last set of very-sick days.

Then I'm sad.

I don't see much that thrills me.

Most of my daily wardrobe now is made up of shapeless black clothing. I can't buy my way into a new "right" wardrobe, and I'm not even sure what "right" means for me. Treadmill-Kasser psychologically winds the desire for the "right" image via clothes with desires for fame and wealth in how they "all share a focus of looking for a sense of worth outside of oneself, and involve striving for external rewards and the praise of others."[19] I don't think I'm looking for praise, per se. And I certainly don't want fame. I just want to feel "right" when I walk into a backyard party or a client meeting.

Is it wrong to want clothes that help me feel right?

"It's a completely arbitrary idea that there's a 'right' way of dressing," Rebecca West tells me. "There is no 'right' when it comes to anything in our home, what we wear, any of it!" Rebecca is an interior designer and the author of Happy Starts at Home. We met through an online workshop she led via my (amazeovaries) hypnotherapist, Iris Higgins, and Rebecca's emotional approach to the human relationship with stuff stayed with me. I feel so lost—at thirty-five!—among the stuff in my space. I can't afford to empty out and refill, and I don't think stuff brings me joy anyway. If it does, I don't know which stuff will!

"Everything of material value—our clothes, our home, our makeup, all of these things—it's like a costume," Rebecca coaches. "It's something you can try on and see how it fits. It's a way of exploring self-identity." She doesn't encourage unnecessary spending (her book helps those on a budget reassess too). And she guides that if we do choose to bring something in, "it should never be something that controls us. It should be something that we're using."

I look at my clothes and take a breath.

Stopping the inward purchasing flow has allowed the panic architecture around this new Challenge to soften too; I'm realizing that it's easier to identify opinions about what I already have when not bringing in more stuff to further clutter the thought process. Looking down, I begin to pinpoint extremes that feel wrong to the "character" I want to be, like the blazers and button-downs that are too business-casual to express my innate creativity or the belts and flowy blouses on the too-hippie end of the spectrum that reek of my former youth. I bin these up for donation. Then some I haven't fit into for a few years but never cared much for to begin with. These cleared, I select a few too-snug beloved items—handmade dresses, vintage skirts, inherited blouses—and make a vow: "If these don't fit by the end of next summer, they go too."

I can now distinguish a *bit* of myself in what remains.

I see someone who blends city and country, earth and sky.

I can daydream a future costume building.

As weeks of the Challenge pass, I let more go out from here and there.

I feel lighter in mind and spirit.

But something doesn't sit right still: the laundry bag. For Rose and Rex, cramming baking supplies in a suitcase helped me whip up wedding cake beachside and ended in a bubbly-fueled, friend-filled Caribbean feast. Hauling the barely usable laundry bag day after day? That only ends in fury.

Should I have bought a new one that first day?

Rebecca's intrigued by my struggle of where to place it on the "essential needs" line. "The essentialness comes from the fact that we live challenging lives," she analyzes. "You have to ask yourself: 'When there are so many challenges in my day I can't control, am I willing to have yet another, with this one little thing I can make *not* an obstacle?'" In not fixing a controllable frustration, we funnel our limited energy away from people who deserve it—our partners, colleagues, and personal wellness practices—giving it instead to nonfunctioning items. "I'm not sure a laundry bag is a great place to put that energy," she says. If we never address such seemingly small frustrations, one layers upon another. We question our self-worth, valuing ourselves among the state of our stuff.

"You *deserved* a new bag," she says gently.

But I'm only halfway through this Challenge.

INVALUABLE

Something is very wrong.

I'm at Bro Dan's again and plugged into my interview comfort zone. On the table in front of me, the screen of my laptop reveals the words my fingers are typing out with speed. My phone is connected to a recorded line where, on the other end, a chef talks me through a recipe; my ears, fingers, eyes, and brain are processing simultaneously. The line records in case I fall behind or stop to converse. But I've done this process hundreds of times before; while interesting, this interview is not particularly difficult.

But my body . . . it's starting to shake?

My heartbeat surges and then falls slow. It floats, flips. Waves of warmth and then cold flood up from my feet through to the top skin of my skull. *What is happening?* I breathe low. I stop typing, focus my eyes on the screen, my ears on his voice, the touch of my fingers resting on the keys. *We're close to the end*, I tell my body. *We've got this.* I cut the goodbye short, keep my voice warm—"Thank you so much!"— and end the call.

I'm shivering?

I race to the back porch and fly into the sun.

What is this?

I think back to my lonely, panicked evening on this same porch a few weeks ago and check my thoughts:

I'm not anxious about work. Or loneliness. Or money.

So, no—this is not emotional anxiety.

This doesn't feel like a familiar swell of pain or fatigue that comes when I've overworked myself into a flare either. I haven't gone suddenly into a "brain fog," where I can't pull words from a dense black cloud.

No.

This is something new.

This feels like the core of my body has shattered, and in the wake of something solid once there, shards are careering into my heart and my stomach, flying out of the pores of my arms and neck and face and hair, making all stand at attention. The ninety-degree heat is doing nothing to soothe this chill.

I take stock to assess if anything I've done might have triggered this. (Always self-blame first. Always.)

What have I eaten today? Did I drink too much coffee?

Did I not take my meds? Accidentally double something?

Has anyone around me been sick lately?

Is my period coming? Is my period late?

Did I not sleep long enough? Did I sleep too much?

I chug two glasses of water. It makes the surge worse.

I eat protein. No difference.

I meditate on my grounding root chakra. Nothing will ground this body.

I hold Mitra close, but her calm makes my soaring more pronounced.

In an interview with *The New York Times*, the writer Laura Hillenbrand describes her physical sensations with myalgic encephalomyelitis—also called chronic fatigue syndrome—like "you're on a ship, and when it's really bad, everything is whirling. I don't know which way is up, and I'm grabbing on to things."[20] I sometimes write about my experience with chronic illness, and so, curious, I survey others, asking them to describe the physical sensations of living in their bodies with illness:

> *"It feels as if the world surrounding me is on fire, and my very core is frozen; my joints are on fire, and yet I sit here, shaking."*

> *"It feels like someone is pulling all of my muscles, from my fingers, to my face, to my legs, neck, and back."*

> *"There's a vise around my head, and it's tightening and closing. I close my eyes and notice the lump in my throat. I quietly ask my heart: Please, dear heart, please stay open, please stay open."*

> *"It feels like I'm wearing an outfit made of lead. I'm splashing and drinking as much water as I can, but I can feel my skin and lips crack. I'm exhausted from trying to get enough water, and the heaviness from the suit hurts every part of me, but I'm still moving."*

> *"It feels like a battlefield, and the enemy is winning."*

Hillenbrand wrote her stunning, intricately researched nonfiction books *Seabiscuit* and *Unbroken* while on her rocking ship. Kat Kinsman has worked her food-writing career with a condition she then documented in her memoir, Hi, *Anxiety*. Esmé Weijun Wang published her novel, *The Border of Paradise*, through late-stage Lyme and schizoaffective disorder. Allie Cashel wrote *Suffering the Silence: Chronic Lyme Disease in an Age of Denial* after years living with Lyme too.

What stormy seas we with illness ride.

Writing in our ships far apart, but pulled on tides, connected.

I force myself to sit and do two more interviews, back-to-back.

I hope my voice sounds interested and engaged.

But all the while my brain echoes:

"Why . . . why . . . why . . . ?"

Then I take a hot shower, medicate, layer in warm clothing, and get back in the sun. I embrace the solitude and let tears stream from my eyes. I want no food, no tending, no company. I let waves of painful sensation move the ship of my body.

I wake the next morning hoping for relief.

But still, the waters rock.

I take three more interviews.

I haven't eaten. But I'm too sick to stomach what I have in the house, and I've removed the nonessential luxury of getting soup or fried rice delivered to my door. I can't *buy* self-sufficiency right now. But is delivery food an essential need in such a circumstance?

"Chronic illnesses interfere with the simple act of feeding oneself in as many ways as there are sicknesses and symptoms," Esmé defines in an article about those facing similar physical limitations. Sometimes the vises and fires and pulls those with chronic illness described exhaust all the energy one needs just to rise from bed, leaving nothing for cooking food. Sometimes a body just can't stomach one thing or another. Sometimes the battle restricts the upright minutes required to pour and heat frozen soup. In such times, Esmé points out, "delivery can be a lifesaver for people living with disability."[21]

She calls it not a luxury, but a "health cost."

I'm too sick in this moment to make an addendum to my rule.

Or are you too stubborn to give in, Jacqueline?

Mom takes up the slack for my indecision.

She comes to check up on me, and worry immediately plasters her face. I pull words from my brain—*fruit, broth, seltzer*—and she goes right back out. The next day a migraine incapacitates me on the couch, and I crouch in fetal position, fighting back vomit, hiding tears, willing the world to stop spinning, and once again powerless to fix things. I've promised my parents that I'm fine—I can manage my responsibilities. But Mom flies in again with migraine meds, broth, and ginger ale. She puts me to bed, pressing cold cloths on my forehead, not leaving until I'm nearly asleep.

I've always prided myself on functional independence, despite illness.

I make clear to my loved ones my burden doesn't have to be theirs.

But then they sweep in and save me when I'm on the floor.

Even if I'm swearing that I can handle things on my own.

I admit now: I can do without such pride.

As the days pass, I realize it's not safe for me to drive for a while. Dad drives me into New York; Mom back to Connecticut. She goes with me to doctors to help strategize the upcoming trip to the Azores with Dad and the *tios*; my siblings help me plan practical steps on the island they also know well. I consider Esmé's "health cost" in regard to essential needs and my body as it is now: weak, changeable, vulnerable.

I decide I can buy very particular stuff for the trip.

I'll be traversing several of the Azores islands. I won't be doing much—riding in cars and resting at our house and in hotels—but I need to double down on comfort. I don't own light, slip-on sneakers; I order a pair of TOMS. I need migraine-defending sunglasses; I find them on sale at a discount store. While there, I splurge on a teeny portable pack that can hold ice or hot water.

Am I *technically cheating on my* No Shopping Challenge?

I barely make it to São Miguel—the flight is short but painful, and the winding roads from the airport to our town hurt at every turn. For the first ten days, I do little but read iPad library books on the front porch of my grandparents' home, now owned by Younger Tío. The glasses block the late summer sun, and the pack keeps my head cool. Every other day The Men drop me at a hotel one town over, where nearby hot springs feed a pool and hot tub. I laze for hours, gazing out through a high wall of windows at the green mountains, pulsing pain but thankful for the restoration my body needs.

One day, Dad and I drive to the top of a high hill to clean our family mausoleum, where my grandparents and great-grandparents and several great-aunts and uncles lie. The cemetery is clean, peaceful. We wipe cobwebs and spiders from silk flowers and picture frames, and sweep the tile floor. Then Dad wanders, paying his respect to friends newly passed, their photographs propped against stone. I sit on the topmost terrace and look out past waving stalks of corn, down over honeysuckle and hydrangea bushes flowerless in this early autumn. I can barely make out the hum of a faraway motorcycle edging around the curved mountain roads and then an old truck engine as it downshifts to pull up a steep incline. Moving anywhere on this island, thrust up as it was so long ago by volcanic force, means always ascending, descending, or anticipating what lies beyond the bend; even the cows moan under the effort. Other than such occasional complaint, it's just me, the breeze, and the Atlantic.

What stories could I pen in such lush isolation? I yearn to capture this landscape, to craft stories of the people living within this curve of sea. But on this trip, I can but breathe life back into my struggling body. A promise: *the next time I set foot here, I will write.*

"The 'health cost' of being ill is especially burdensome to many already struggling financially," concludes Esmé.

I try not to take into account the cost of my health during this time.

Not as we hop three more islands and The Men explore while I read in my hotel room, accepting the forced isolation my body demands. Not in their contributing equal parts cash to pay for our four-party bills, their deep-rooted familial generosity thinly veiling my poverty and shame. Not when I return home, and the money I've saved during this Challenge goes to doctors and prescriptions, as I try to figure out just why my body changed that day and why it doesn't revert back to baseline. Not in the continued income loss, as it's weeks before my racing body slows, my mind clears, and I can sit in front of a screen and work again.

I try, instead, to think of how Dad picked up the phone when I called him from the porch that day and said how much he loved me. How FW Lyndsey, struggling through her own illness, talked me through how to get to the couch. How Mom kept showing up, despite how often I swore that I could manage on my own. How Younger Tio surprised me with a plane ticket to the Azores. How Older Tio insisted they take care of me on a trip I needed more than ever. And of the warm water and green mountains of my precious São Miguel.

These are invaluable.

RECALCULATING

PHYSICAL HEALTH: I need to flip the story I've been telling myself for too long: flares of illness are not only a part of my past. I need to save as if one might be around the corner. Swearing that "I can handle this myself!" doesn't mean I can. Accepting help doesn't make me a lesser person or mean that I've given up hope I might one day be "healthy" for good. And paying to get things delivered to my door is not always a luxury. Sometimes it's survival.

SOCIAL INTERACTIONS: I now better understand how to prioritize worthy experiential purchases. I didn't spend twenty-five dollars for a silent movie at the Cathedral of Saint John the Divine on Halloween weekend because I'd experienced this thrill before; I did buy twenty-dollar discounted tickets for my roommate, Erika, and me to see two Christmas shows coming up in December(!). Buying a cup of coffee because I'm killing time in Brooklyn after the radio show is "shopping"; chipping in for shots at Lizzie's thirtieth birthday shindig, even though I'm not drinking, is a contribution to one of my dearest relationships.

SENSE OF SELF: In taking the time to stop and wager practical and emotional value, I better understand the *stuff* in my life. Shedding clothes, books, and makeup I don't use, I'm closer to my elusive "right." I start to feel *me* through the fog.

***

5,942 padded mattress covers sit ready for purchase on Amazon.com. 5:57 a.m. on October 30, my fingers hunt for just the right one.

A few minutes ago, the trill of drunken neighbors stumbling down the street below my window had yanked me out of REM cycle. Infuriated, I tried to trick my brain to sleep with breathing patterns and meditative mind games, until lost in torment, I started to ponder the comfort of a cushy mattress topper. My brain fixed upon the date: in precisely eighteen hours and three delicious minutes, I can buy whatever I want again! But if more comfortable, it'll be harder for outside stimulation to wake me. This makes a mattress topper an essential health cost. I can buy it now!

Satisfied by logic, I scroll and click, iPhone light blasting and Mitra burrowing under the sheets as if to take no part in the scheme.

By 6:15 a.m., my neglected debit card stands ready, and if I just make one more click, the prize will start making its way toward my door.

I stop. I put down the phone. I sigh into the darkness.

I know this click-fix won't quick-fix my situation.

It worked—I've reset my shopping habit.

Dammit.

In the last ninety days, I have not bought a single book. Other than the documented TOMS and a bra (I was about to leave for the Azores without one!), I haven't bought clothes. I bought one to-go coffee when I was out of beans and *needed* a jolt. I bought one candle after I'd burned all others. I bought tinted lip balm, but no other makeup. I reduced grocery items to essentials, adding only a two-dollar carton of lemonade (once you have that fresh-squeezed taste) and a pint of dairy-free ice cream (I was writing about the company, and it was on sale). I trimmed spending by way of on-demand movies, holding back at dinners or not dining out at all, and accepting boredom instead of distracting with unneeded stops for coffee or a snack.

I faced dozens of tiny inconveniences.

But also great emotional wins.

Having cleared out some stuff I decidedly don't love, I'm enjoying refreshed space. But I can now also identify the worn-down practical items I cannot do without—my computer, my furniture, my vacuum—but also not afford to replace, and my patchwork home looks progressively faded. "When things become shabby around you . . . you really start to question your sense of self-worth," Happy-Home Rebecca worries. "Like, 'I guess I deserve to live like this.'" This makes sense to me. But I'm starting to hope that this Year will deliver on the long game of self-discovery. And while I can technically shop again, I decide I'll try to get comfortable among my bit of shab; I'll continue to explore my self-worth aside from the stuff around me.

(Maybe that's the point of this *without* journey?) Because I need more energy, and I'll save it if I have less excess stuff to tend.

Yes.

Going without Shopping, I now better understand *want* versus *need*:

I want but don't need more stuff, even if it does bring me joy.

I want but don't need the "right" look.

I want but don't need the social limelight.

I want but don't need to always work so hard.

I want but don't need to always fix my problems on my own.

I do need more energy so to move forward my single-sick-broke trifecta.

I do need to invest more in the communities I'm only just rediscovering.

I do need more physical comfort in my body and far better health overall.

I do need to trust that my loved ones will love me, no matter how often I call on them for help.

I do need more confidence in myself and my abilities.

I need a greater sense of grounding in who I am.

I need a far stronger stock of inner peace.

And an unflappable bank of resilience.

I can't buy these things.

I can only cultivate them within.

CHAPTER **3**
CHALLENGE

NO SUGAR

CHALLENGE: No Sugar

TIME LINE: Thirty days

RULES: I will not eat refined or natural sugars, including honey, corn syrup, molasses, agave, coconut nectar, etc., or sugar substitutes. I will not eat corn, but other (gluten-free) starchy foods are okay. I will not eat fruit. I will not drink alcohol.

UNSWEETENED

In September, *JAMA Internal Medicine* published documents revealing that back in the 1960s the Sugar Research Foundation (now the Sugar Association) helped to falsify studies on the dangers of eating fat.[22] CEOs threw money at scientists, scientists skewed data, and for decades following, marketing campaigns then encouraged us to scarf low-fat foods saturated with extra sweet in the name of our good health. Those who sold the sweet stuff got rich; those who ate got obesity, heart disease, and diabetes.

57

Or so the story goes in the flood of think pieces following JAMA's reveal.[23]

I want my next Challenge to push the physical health parameter I set out in My Year, Without rules, and so I ponder my relationship with sugar. While I don't have a stereotypical addiction, I adore sweets as treats. Reading Isabel Allende on São Miguel, I crunched away at café meringues until my sticky fingers were licked clean. At home, a sliver of gluten-free brownie often accompanies a good single-gal *Gilmore Girls* binge-in-bed—there's definitely a feeling of *reward* in the loop here. Angsty food-writer work events often require a wine crutch, and dating practically demands booze. So going without habitual consumption of sugar (and the sugar inherent in alcohol) would satisfy social interaction parameters too. And then there's a clear sense-of-self struggle I'm almost afraid to face head-on: I detest the extra pounds I carry.

A year or so before Ruark and I broke up, life teemed with health, work, and energy. Then—poof. In a short span of time, I fell lost to illness again. I could no longer work and so quit my jobs. My theater company produced shows without me. My parents provided financial support. As I was too sick to go out, a few loyal friends trekked over for game nights. The rest sort of … friend-ghosted. I wasted away in spirit, and pounds wasted from my body; in sickness, it loathed food, despite how much I pushed to nourish it. I don't look back at this time with fond remembrance. But as a tailor took in my pants and I received regular compliments on the dramatic loss, I felt secret pleasure in outward drama matching interior strife. I bought those smaller-size clothes. I tilted my face in the mirror to admire the pronounced curve of my jawline. I knew I was underweight. I loved food. I would have done anything to get back to living. But being skinny was *something*.

Today, I'm sick without the skinny reward, overweight the amount I was underweight before. It feels like I'm stuck inside a puffy me-suit, one that comes with me into every dressing room, every cocktail party, and every speaking engagement. As a feminist and rational thinker, I despise myself for falling prey to such superficial strife.

I can't be the only woman struggling with this.

I take the conundrum in story form to Bust magazine.[24] For my research, I conduct an informal online survey with 285 women who identify losing or gaining weight because of illness. Eighty percent report an adverse effect on their body image. Across the board, those who lost weight recount being praised for it; those who gained, shamed. Reflections range from "It felt like I was preconditioned to feel a grim satisfaction as I watched the pounds slip away" to "I don't look into mirrors anymore."

I then interview Dr. Erin I. Kleifield, a psychologist and the director of the eating disorders program at Silver Hill Hospital in New Canaan, Connecticut. Why do I struggle with this particular weight shift and identity conflict? She explains that our brain pushes us toward anything we think will move us higher on the social survival ladder; as described by Kasser's hedonic treadmill, striving for thinness is rooted in a society that constantly blasts us with images of successful thin models and celebrities. The loss of our health makes us feel powerless; we then loathe our lack of control over rational thought too. "We need to be aware, and we need to bring in compassion," she says.

I easily feel compassion for those in my Bust story.

Self-compassion comes harder.

Like many others surveyed, I carry an exorbitant amount of guilt inside my me-suit, sure I must be feeding or denying my body something it needs and, therefore, it continually punishes me with pain. I have reason to fear this; Lyme disease remains one of the most misunderstood diseases of my lifetime.[25] Accurate diagnosis and effective treatment were even more unreliable when I was first diagnosed in the early 1990s than they are today. Because we don't yet know why some patients remain symptomatic post-treatment, many doctors pass what they cannot cure over to the realm of psychiatry. Despite confirmative blood work and treatment a second time, I often face suspicion of my mental health from medical professionals. On a recent first visit, a new doctor wouldn't even look at my records; instead, she concluded twelve minutes into our consultation that my ongoing pain and fatigue stem from depression, despite lab work in my hands charting healthy dopamine and serotonin levels. I know too many with similar stories of misdiagnosis and distrust. Gender bias in medical care often leaves women particularly untreated:[26] in comparable circumstances with men, we are more likely to die in the ICU and to be given sedatives over painkillers.[27] Established racial bias[28] further harms nonwhite women: Black women are less likely to have breast cancer than white women but 40 percent more likely to die from it,[29] and black and Hispanic women are up to three times more likely to have lupus,[30] yet go longer before diagnosis all because of systems that limit education, access, and options.

To reduce any chance of fault, I've spent years working my body through the Atkins Diet, the Ketogenic Diet, the Arthritis Diet, the ALCAT Test—all of which remove sugar. I've done several elimination diets, too, where you reset your digestive system's inflammatory response and then incrementally add foods back to identify which cause symptoms. I spend months eating alone for these, poring over lists and obsessing over minuscule changes. From them all, I've learned much about how food affects my symptoms and overall health. But my enigma of a disease is not easily Sherlocked, and none cured the source.

I've spent years of my life fielding guilt for self-harm I haven't committed.

And every failed attempt scars me against hope.

But this Year has proven change can come from unexpected places.

Maybe going without sugar again will shift something unexplored?

For thirty days, I will not eat refined or natural sugars. I will not drink alcohol. Sticking to self-imposed simplicity, I'll allow the dairy or carbs other sugar abstainers might argue I should also quit. Because this Year is about going without one thing at a time; throwing one stone, not tossing pebbles.

I want change within my body.

I want change within my reflection.

I will try.

WITHDRAWAL

Day One. Time to take a cold, hard look at my drinking habits.

I make some strong coffee—thank *dog* my favorite brand of almond milk contains no sugar or sneaky successor ending in *ose* (fructose, galactose, etc.)! I hit the computer. Five color-coded digital calendars differentiate life responsibilities, piecing together what my brain could never recall on its own. I print out last month and get my pen ready. I check **Xs** for drinking nights and circle large **Os** around when I was blissfully *not sober anymore.*

Sixteen **Xs**. Five large **Os.**

In one week, alcohol had entered my bloodstream on five evenings. I sit with this.

None of those nights involved embarrassment, vomit, or dramatically regretful decisions. The **X** often stood for only a glass. But I'm apparently in denial at the ease at which I self-medicate against social interactions or the crap end of a long day. And now, I'm using "self-medicate" to justify my actions out of self-conscious shame.

What will life be like without booze?

This would be easier to face with a brownie in hand.

I have an all-day date planned with a guy I'll call . . . RoboWriter. (For anonymity, here on out men met in some romantic context will be given a *crude nom de guerre*. This guy is former military and a writer.) We've been dating for twenty-four days now, and we met because I couldn't buy a cup of coffee during the No Shopping Challenge. No joke.

Ben and I had just wrapped a show with Rashied Amini, who founded Nanaya, a dating algorithm that suggests where you're most likely to find compatible mates given your social habits, values, etc. In prep, I'd run Nanaya on myself and was crushed to learn my odds are best online. Easily convinced, there I was after the show: killing time in Roberta's backyard before a Tinder date, unable to buy the nonessential cup of coffee I *wanted* from next door, and bored. I scrolled OKCupid, found RoboWriter, and before I knew it we had dinner plans for two nights later. The thing is, I already had a *third* date planned for Friday with Mr. Meet-Cute, who I'd met in Connecticut when out not drinking tequila shots on Lizzie's birthday.

A week later I was exhausted and confused.

Three first dates with men different in profession, intellect, emotion, and physicality. Three perfectly lovely evenings of dinner and conversation. Three goodnight kisses I confess to slightly phoning in. Three invitations for second dates; a freak occurrence if there ever was one. Eventually, timing and charm had me choose RoboWriter: he's cute, smart, and a nerd in the hottest sense of the word. We've talked books, dined through Manhattan, overnighted in Brooklyn, and slowly opened to each other.

Today, a work-pleasure date will end at my place.

For the first time.

Without alcohol.

It's a crisp New York fall day; sorta wet and sorta cold and not the kind I'd prefer to spend moving from one place to the next. But RoboWriter's a workaholic and seems to admire that part of me, so my ego pushes me to impress. He watches me prerecord a radio interview with an author we both admire. Then we grab Chinese and nosh on a park bench. (Cantonese takeout might save me during this Challenge.) Late afternoon, we settle into the Rose Room to write. But his muscly, tattooed arms and the screeching of my joints distract, I'm fading in the absence of adrenaline lost to interview, conversation, and traversing streets and subways. I ignore my body's call to go home alone and, kissing him on the head in a gesture of easy affection I'm excited to try, whisper I'm off to grab dinner supplies. I stock up on scallops and spices, grab us both a coffee, and burn under the weight of recording equipment, my ancient laptop, and groceries as we subway uptown.

I hide my pain. I like him. I want to appear strong.

I sit him in my kitchen with tequila and perform my seduction dinner around him. He doesn't know I call it this, of course, but I run some variation of this show when trying to impress a dude I like. My feet are bare, and my apron is tied tight. I casually whip sunchokes and fry fritters. In the past, I'd break to sip or quickly canoodle. But it's late. The muscles around my spine burn. As I sear the scallops and toss spicy arugula with oil and pepper, I realize we're not flirting. RoboWriter is smart and cute and—*damn*—I haven't liked anyone since the porch guy last summer. I sense he seeks deep discussion, but I can barely keep casual conversation. I slip into a neurological haze and—*shit*—my thoughts muddle like the spices I pound together in my mortar.

This is why there are so many Xs on the calendar, Jacqueline.

A wine haze delays this decline so that others don't have to deal with this part of me. So that I can be more fun, flirtier. So that wit and words matter less. If alone, I'd sink into the tub. I'd melt into bed, self-soothing with the flat screen, a heating pad, and Mitra. I'd let the pain come.

But I'm not alone. I don't know how to date sick *and* sugar free.

Last week, tarot reader and author Sasha Graham came on to *Love Bites*. "It's interesting, the things that come up for us in our lifetime," she said after I filled her in on similar symptoms and dating worries. "You're a wordsmith. This is your life and your passion. For something to strike at the heart of that . . . it can't be easy." She pulled the Knight of Swords from her deck and suggested I envision myself held up by its beautiful suit of steel; clear in thought and intent, I am the hero of my story.

I don't tell RoboWriter how I'm feeling: I don't know how he'll react and feel too sick to risk vulnerability. I'll try when stronger. For now, I envision my suit. For now, I finish cooking. We eat. I phone in sex. We sleep.

After I announced this Challenge, one online friend shared that she'd passed out after only eight hours off of sugar. Another had suffered massive headaches for four days straight. My Day Three, I put RoboWriter on the subway and breathe out in relief. I could devour an entire pint of sorbet, but I recognize that I'm overtired, in pain, and dehydrated, and put extra lemon in my water instead. The next night, a spiced tea satisfies a want for something sweet. I make it past the withdrawal mark without any dramatic reaction.[31]

Maybe I will just coast through this one.

Day Five. Election Night 2016. The country hums.

I've been invited to parties around Manhattan. But since I can't drink or dine with the best of them, I make tea and cuddle Mitra in the warm living room light, alone. I note projections: seven major analysts, from the Associated Press to the *Los Angeles Times*, predict a sweeping victory for Hillary Clinton. The AP gives her lowest-odds 274 Electoral College votes to Donald Trump's projected 190.[32] Friends text, already tippling champagne for Clinton's historic win. I light candles, content with tea and temperance.

Shortly after seven o'clock, Trump takes Indiana and Kentucky while Clinton takes Vermont; nothing surprising there. New York votes Clinton, and the Empire State Building blasts blue.[33] Among headlines revealing endless lines and voter suppression, Clinton gets Massachusetts, New Jersey, and Maryland, and Texas goes to Trump.[34]

9:45 p.m., something is . . . off.

Trump already has 145 electoral votes and is showing well in Florida, North Carolina, Virginia, and Ohio, battleground states Clinton needs. She still leads, but victory is not guaranteed. I stare, dumbfounded, as the scene collapses, my sweet little sweet-less ritual collapsing with it. Trump gets Missouri, then Ohio. My jaw grinds. Clinton gets Virginia and Colorado, but then Trump Florida.[35] My stomach knots. I scan social media and read similar shock and woe fueled or numbed by alcohol.

With a blow to the gut I realize:

I cannot grab the bottles on the bar across the room.

I cannot pull the brownies from my freezer.

I never took this scenario into Challenge consideration!

I *take it back*!

No. I don't.

I warm a plate of food. I make more tea.

I hope nourishment will suffice.

It doesn't.

I watch as the future shifts in a way my brain cannot comprehend. I sit and take it, on my couch, alone. Trump gets North Carolina . . . I want an entire bottle of white wine. If Clinton can get Michigan, Pennsylvania, New Hampshire, Nevada . . . I want an entire chocolate cake or a stiff martini—the ingredients sit ready, only ten feet away. It would be so easy to raise the white flag and give in. *I want to raise the white flag and give in*! I need something to take off this edge, to self-soothe, to wrap my insides in a hug. I am horribly, painfully alone. I'm *lonely*. I'm angry at my body for not being strong enough, so I could spend this significant evening with others. I'm hurt RoboWriter doesn't give a shit enough to be in touch today. I'm disappointed that loved ones who know I'm alone haven't checked in. And, more than anything, I'm furious with myself for not handling this better! Evidently, I did *not* learn a lesson in solitude and self-reliance when I went off social media!

I take Mitra for a walk. I look up at the sky. I breathe.

"The stars have seen worse," I comfort myself.

"You are safe," I comfort myself.

We come back inside.

At 2:30 a.m. on November 9, the Associated Press announces that Hillary Clinton has conceded the forty-fifth presidency of the United States of America to Donald Trump.[36] In the weeks to come, I'll join the mass of clichéd white liberals pushed from our temperate social bubbles to join those who've never had a choice but to fight for themselves. Of course, I don't know this yet. Right now I'm just sober and stunned.

As I move forward from Election Day, I consider coping mechanisms.

Through Hypnotherapist-Higgins again, I recently took an online workshop with narrative medicine instructor Micaela Bombard called The Body Speaks. Exhausted from living in my mine, I wrote this during a two-minute exercise inviting us to write a love letter to one specific body part:

> Dear right pinky finger,
>
> I don't think about you much. I mean that as the highest compliment because that means you don't hurt me. You're on my stronger hand. You don't swell. I don't wear rings on you, and you're not vital for writing, cooking, carrying, or anything, really, that I can think of. I honestly don't know what I would do if I lost you because I don't think of you. And for that, I am thankful. I love you, right hand pinky finger. You're my favorite body part today. I am naming you Happy. You just made me smile. I like your fingernail. After this phone call, I am going to paint it. Just yours. Probably *before* the end of this phone call, after I put the phone back on mute. Just you. Thanks, Happy. Time hasn't run out yet, so I'm going to o n l y t y p e w i t h y o u n o w, H a p p y...

Postelection, Happy doesn't distract for more than a few passing seconds.

I cry over coffee with Roomie Erika. I cry, cuddling Mitra in my corner chair. I cry, watching Clinton's concession speech. I cry on the phone with Mom—Nana fell and is in the hospital with a broken hip and fractured shoulder. I cry at my desk, losing time to the rain. I stress about family and lapsing deadlines as I rotate coffee and water. I don't give a damn about food. I pretend not to give a damn that RoboWriter is still acting gauzy. A part of me wishes I could drink away my pain; another is relieved I'm not hungover on top of all this.

Maybe it's better to be sober during hard times?

Maybe barreling through bad is the fastest way to good?

Finally, a text! RoboWriter's work schedule has changed, and he invites me to join him for dinner. Sweet comfort, yes!

I scramble downtown in the still-misting rain. My step lightens as I pass under massive stone archways and into the courtyard of his building. I'm nervous and excited. I settle under the romantic streetlamp glow a dozen feet from where, two weeks ago, he welcomed me with a comforting hug after I showed up exhausted. Today, he's the one walking low; I can't imagine this election is easy on a liberal writer in law enforcement. He offers a quick peck, then collapses on to the stone by my side. The air hangs heavy between us, our fears shared. I want to hold his body to mine as we start to talk it out, but his posture doesn't invite this. And so I offer space. He starts venting concern for those in military and public office— friends and colleagues—steering from one facet to another, his body tense. I don't have solutions to soothe him. But I have spent my life navigating realities out of my control. And so I listen. As best I can, I guide him through thoughts and feelings. I nurture. Twenty minutes pass. He stands to face me.

"You are such an amazing woman . . ."

—my heart lifts—

" . . . but I'm just not feeling a spark."

I don't realize I'm holding my breath until I force my lungs to exhale.

He starts to apologize, to excuse. I keep my gaze steady as he rambles: he doesn't know why he feels this way. He's told his friends I'm perfect on paper, but he can't figure out why he doesn't feel long-term potential. He'd needed a few days to assess but could tell I sensed his pulling away. He didn't want to do this via text and finds talking on the phone barbaric, which is why he asked me to come down here. He hopes we stay in touch. He offers his connections in publishing. He's sorry and . . .

I nod and keep my voice low, contemplating both his concern and condescension: *It's okay. Don't beat yourself up. Sometimes there's no logic. Better to move on sooner than later. We're good.* He calms.

We stand in silence. There's nothing more to say.

We move back under the now-oppressive stone. We hit the avenue.

For the first time, he doesn't walk me to my train.

Instead, we awkwardly hug.

He turns left; I continue straight.

And he's gone.

I walk forward, navigating slowly. Somehow, still breathing.

Everything before me looks a little different than it did an hour ago.

Two days later.

One hundred and forty-five days of going without.

I stand in the shower, sobbing.

A man who mocks fundamental human rights is president-elect.

A man I was emotionally warming to rejected me.

Sweetheart Nana's body is broken and sweetheart Poppa beside himself.

Sweetheart mother has a long road in tending to them.

I barely made deadlines this week.

I overtaxed my body in the drive to make them.

I've cried so much my right eye is infected.

I feel pathetic and insignificant and deserted and afraid.

My body folds over in angular origami.

I dig gnarled fingers into my flesh.

I don't want to feel this!

"Please tell me this misery is sugar withdrawal?"

I reach out to Dr. Nicole Avena, a neuroscientist and researcher who studies hedonic eating; eating for reasons other than hunger. She explains sugar is a stimulant that releases dopamine (that happy neurotransmitter) in the brain; when we get addicted to the happy rush and remove the source, we then crave it and go into withdrawal.[37] Prior to this Challenge, I had been feeding my brain sugar through fruit, wine, occasional desserts, and trace amounts in things like mayonnaise and restaurant meals. Having removed such compounded sources, I almost hope that my brain is screaming for a dopamine hit, making life circumstances *feel* exponentially worse than they are.

We're only projecting here, but I want her best guess: Is this physiological or psychological?

"We've seen in our studies that people who are casual sugar eaters or on a regularly low-sugar diet don't show that opioid response," Dr. Avena explains. "Based on what you're telling me about your diet history, it was more a psychological component," she concludes. She calls my wine and brownies "little indulgences"—not responses to brain cravings. I show easy judgment and restraint otherwise and had no direct physical symptoms after I removed them, so her studies suggest sugar has not altered my brain in such a way that I have gone into a severely disturbed withdrawal mode from the loss.

This isn't sugar. This is life.

And so . . . I ask my body to process. To accept.

Years of unreliable health, failed romance, and job insecurity have encouraged habits of emotional survival; like putting mere bandages on wounds that needed stitching. I allow the sum reality to soak in: the anger, loneliness, fear, and helplessness I can't remember feeling in such depths before, let alone all at once.

I didn't expect airing wounds to hurt this much.

Anthropologist-Amber lectures, "There's this thing where women joke, 'Oh, it's a bad day. I'll drink wine.' Stop! You're covering up the fact that you are miserable . . . Allow yourself to be miserable. Allow yourself to hate yourself and to start to like yourself again. Monitor all those bad-thoughts loops."

Loops can go suck lollipops.

But I *can* do this.

I *can* face unexpected experiences.

And so, I face this: I'm crumbling.

LOSER

Dr. Kleifield's voice shoots into my brain from out of nowhere: "Check your motivation."

She halts the sensation of Mr. Meet-Cute's lips dragging against mine.

This does not make me happy.

Well, I am happy about one thing.

His hands are running up my trimmed waistline.

It's Day Fourteen, and I've lost seven pounds.

I haven't been cooking much since my (failed) RoboWriter seduction dinner. I'm eating my first meal later every day, surviving Lorelai-like on "Coffee! Coffee! Coffee!" and handfuls of cashews. I down chicken broth for sustenance and maybe grab potato chips between subway platforms if lightheaded in transit. But overwhelming hunger has fled. I suspect the loss comes more from an overall drop in calories than sugar absence. Or that it's not real weight loss, and it'll come back when this Challenge or mood or *whatever* ends. I don't care. After weathering RoboWriter's rejection, no-strings sex with an acquaintance technically scratched an itch but was so boringly bad I immediately questioned *that* motivation, indeed. Then Mr. Meet-Cute reached out, confessing he was more forlorn by my walking away than he'd originally let on. Like a proper balm for my crumbling self-worth, I hope kismet forgives my having chosen wrong.

I'd flushed with minxy-smug satisfaction at his eyes taking in my thinner frame as we walked into the dive bar. Now he's drinking solo and kissing away all my melodramatic mental woe.

Who needs food? Who needs booze?

I allow myself to feel *hot* for a hot second.

Again, Dr. Kleifield: "Where is this voice coming from?"

Dammit! It's not *her* voice she's referring to.

Meet-Cute goes for another beer.

I reapply gloss and check in with my subconscious.

Back in that interview, I'd asked her how to identify when you're dieting for better health versus solely to get thin: "This is where you ask your intuitive self: 'Where is this coming from?'" she'd coached. "Is it punishing or is it a voice that wants to help you? Only you can tell what that voice is."

I've carried body loathing for quite a while, and with so much about my life I can't control at present, now might be the time when I'd let this No Sugar Challenge give me an excuse to jump down an unhealthy rabbit hole. Am I *telling* myself I'm not hungry? I . . . don't know. So far, no danger signs flash. But to be safe, I decide to monitor my appetite and pump in healthier things than coffee and potato chips. And as I steer Meet-Cute and me toward food, I commend myself at least for not spending another night crying in the shower.

As time passes, I eat a little more and continue to lose weight.

I sleep more soundly at night, but tack that to a lack of booze haze.

Nothing else changes.

My skin isn't clearer. My headaches don't ebb. My body pain remains.

Curiosity has me seeking out Dr. Thomas Brunoski, whom Mom found a few months after my initial Lyme diagnosis. As I navigate Lil' Blue up the eerily familiar office drive, childhood memories lost to waiting room chairs, IV needles, and ceaseless pain flood in. I remember paddling YMCA pools with senior citizens while friends navigated seventh grade. And long hours in bed, staring through the window at trees, waiting for Dad to come home and carry me to the television. This mild PTSD clouds memories of even the best doctor ghosts of treatments past.

Back then, Dr. B immediately took me off a torturously endless list of foods believed to cause inflammation, pumped me full of vitamins, and I credit his building up my immune system as to why I could eventually walk again. (Yeah, it was that bad.)

He helped "cure" me.

Yet here I am: twenty-plus years later, still searching for answers.

But Dr. B smiles wide as we settle into his comfortably aged office. "It is wonderful to see you again!" he starts. "You live life and wonder, and then you see someone from years ago. It's like family returning! It's great."

Without hesitation, he jumps into how healthful eating isn't a mysterious, complicated construct the wellness world muddles today. "Our bodies are made of three things: water, protein, and fat," he explains. "We've got to supply them, and the rest are optional. What we're *not* made out of are sugar and other carbohydrates."

To oversimplify: sugar—including any sweet, starchy, or dairy-full food—breaks down in the blood to glucose, which is what we commonly hear called our "blood sugar levels." As blood sugar levels rise, the pancreas secretes insulin to drop the blood sugar levels back down again. Insulin is called the "master controlling hormone" because it raises inflammatory hormones like leukotriene and eicosanoids, which trigger cortisol (the lovely stress hormone). These further prompt inflammation and weight gain. So the more you give insulin a chance to play in your body, the more inflammation and weight you struggle to manage.

On top of this, there's the hypoglycemia I've struggled with since my first diagnosis. Hypoglycemia is called "insulin resistance" or "low blood sugar." The converse of diabetes (where the pancreas doesn't secrete insulin), with hypoglycemia the pancreas puts out *too much* insulin, causing blood sugar levels to drop too low. We feel a blood sugar crash, our bodies signal us to eat (something sugary) to bring levels back up, and the cycle repeats. "Your appetite surges, you get shaky, adrenaline surges," Dr. B describes. "It's like a vicious machine. It just keeps going." So all of this insulin stuff is especially bad news bears for people with both hypoglycemia *and* inflammatory conditions like mine. Dr. B suspects if I restart the Challenge, removing all starchy foods completely, and go at it for a longer amount of time, I'll see reduced inflammation in my joint pain and mild rosacea.

I leave his office energized and ready to rumble!

Then I remind myself: I've done such promising diets before. My Year is about taking out, taking off, and lightening the load. I'm removing habits on a scale I can dissect and marking changes. That's all. I have to keep on point.

A few days later, I'm still chewing on this insulin stuff (and Cape Cod 40% Reduced Fat Potato Chips). So: I've cut out sugar and fruit, but *not* starchy foods. A doctor I was with for many years said test results consistently suggest I have a "lazy liver," where fructose is largely digested. I have celiac disease—an autoimmune disorder triggered when gluten hits the intestines (another organ essential for digesting fructose)—and other intestinal issues.

Do I have a problem digesting fructose more than glucose?

How touchy is this whole system?

I get Gary Taubes on the phone. He's a science journalist who tracks sugar in articles and his books, *Good Calories, Bad Calories* and *Why We Get Fat*. Like Dr. Avena, he stresses that we're just hypothesizing; science only gets us so far. (*I get it, you guys!*) He reiterates Dr. Brunoski's assertion about insulin; as the hormone most directly related to fat, it plays into my scenario no matter the instigator. Then, because I ask him to, he *Blood Sugar for Dummies* what I've read in his books.

All sugar converts into triglycerides: they get stored in fat cells while the pancreas secretes insulin and starts knocking blood sugar levels down. Once the blood sugar level gets to a "trigger point," some of those triglycerides break down into fatty acids and go back into the bloodstream, where they burn as energy. The unused remain indefinitely in the fat cells. "Endocrinologists who study this refer to your fat tissue as being exquisitely sensitive to insulin," Taubes explains. "A tiny bit of insulin holds on to fat; below that bit, it doesn't."

The turn of the screw is that there is no definition for "tiny bit." "Tiny bit" changes from person to person. "Tiny bit" is why I eat two dark chocolate peanut butter cups and look like a squirrel because my insulin goes haywire and why a member of the Sell family across the street eats the same and *loses* weight.

"The average person, making an effort, burns about thirty to fifty grams of carbs per day," Dr. Brunoski had told me. "That's making an effort, going to the gym. That's one or two thin slices of bread or a small potato. That's it—for the *day*."

As someone who does not make an effort, I probably handle a minuscule bit of insulin before the triglycerides in my fat cells stay there indefinitely. Toss hypoglycemia in the mix and who knows how low the threshold? But I eat at *least* thirty-six grams of carbohydrates via my potato chips![38] I ask Taubes: Could removing only fructose chill my system out? He reiterates that the studies behind sugar aren't specific enough to give me an answer. Or, as proven by the JAMA reveal, they're often too skewed to be trusted.

I yearn for specifics. But in the wake of superior science, my supersmart experts say self-improvement is for the individual to figure out.

That's what I'm doing, this Year, Without.

SOBERED

Meet-Cute drops whiskey into a glass for himself.

With only a few days to go before this Challenge ends, I again don't have alcohol to soften my edges and am still not feeling "right." But we just shared a lovely dinner, then walked to his apartment with arms linked. Now, he grabs his drink and slowly shows me around. First, his music collection, his art. His space is so clean and curated—so unlike RoboWriter's nerdy gruff—and I wonder if we try on relationships like Happy-Home Rebecca costumes too? He shows me his bedroom. I let out a relieved breath when he doesn't protest my walking back out again.

I pull a blanket to his couch, cold in my dress and tights, and settle in.

We watch a movie. I pretend not to notice how often he gets up to refill. Or how he doesn't ask if I need anything. Or how close he puts his body next to mine when he returns. (I want him close . . .

right?) As soon as credits roll, he starts kissing me, hard. His body feels overwarm against mine. His breath mingles beer, whiskey, and salt. I kiss back out of . . . politeness? I'm holding him off more than inviting him in, and I'm not sure why. (Do I even *like* him?) It's after midnight, I'm tired and sore, and I'm trying to decide which way I should move this from the haze of my brain when he mumbles, wetly, directly into my mouth:

"So can Lyme disease be spread sexually?"

I pull back, confused.

I haven't told him about my health issues.

He sees my shock, explains he read it in one of my articles.

I shouldn't be surprised—it happens frequently. Designer-Amber points out that our cyborgs live available to all, at any time, without our knowledge or approval. But I'm sort of pissed he brought it up in this moment, when I'm in his apartment and couldn't be more vulnerable.

(Or relieved for an excuse to pull my lips from his.)

I stay for what feels like a socially appropriate amount of unemotional conversation on my part and a kind but somewhat drunkenly inarticulate response on his. Then it's time to go. I refuse the car he offers. Ever polite, he insists on walking me to the subway. He asks me out again before a final kiss. I say yes, so I can make this night end. But something in me knows I want this date to be our last. I ride an almost-empty subway car, pondering thanks for self-enforced sobriety.

Would tonight have ended differently if I had been drinking too?

I carry this Challenge past the thirty-day finish line, overlapping the next and into the holidays. Day Thirty-Seven, festively celebrating with my Photographer Friend Brent, the first sip of Vermentino rushes pleasure to every nerve. I savor the rounded palate and bouquet of the first glass; the second lasts even longer and the dark alleyway bar falls into a soft blur. I accept a sip of Brent's red, then return to water and small bites of food.

I get home early, walk Mitra, fall into bed.

What fun! What friendship! Hi-ho for holidays! No harm done!

I sleep hard.

3:00 a.m.—*bang!*—and I awake to a cymbal crash of migraine and fever.

My joints beg to be ripped from their sockets.

I strip naked, chug water, and writhe.

My head pounds, my body burns. I watch the clock tick.

The next day, head and bed distract at every turn.

Is this all from two glasses of white wine?

"It's sugar *and* alcohol *and* no doubt a toxic reaction to the so-called congeners in the wine," Dr. Brunoski lectures. Despite my title as "food writer," I've never heard of these "congeners," and I immediately despise them. E*vidently*, they're biologically active byproducts of the fermentation process; the tannins that come from grape skins and give wine much of its complexity and antioxidants. White wine has fewer congeners than red, but is not entirely innocent. "You get to the point when you ask yourself an objective question," Dr. B says. "Are we having fun yet? You get pleasure out of many other things. You don't have to intoxicate yourself."

I'm only thirty-five. I don't want to stop drinking entirely. I tell him so.

He patiently advises then that I try high-quality vodka, which has the fewest congeners and lowest sugar out of most tested forms of alcohol. I pocket the suggestion and continue my search for answers.

Dr. Avena and Taubes also can't differentiate if sugar or alcohol was the main culprit. Taubes says scientists don't even agree as to if they metabolize the same way in the liver. Both conclude my reaction was most likely a matter of acclimation; I was out of practice metabolizing and reintroduced at a high volume. "I bet if you had two glasses the next day, you wouldn't have had the same effect," Dr. Avena ponders.

I'm so afraid to try that it's two *weeks* before I make a second attempt.

I have a first date with a guy so handsome and boring we'll call him Clark Kent. I show up first to a French jazz club in the East Village, take a banquette, and ask for their best vodka in a martini. They only serve French wine and beer. Of course. I order a French Chardonnay. Clark arrives. He's charming. I'm charming. We eat a little. He moves next to me on the banquette to "see the music." We talk with fingers entwined. I order a second glass. He orders a beer. He kisses me. I like it. I stop drinking. He holds my umbrella above us as we walk up 1st Avenue, tight under rain that bounces off the concrete. We kiss by the subway. Clark heads east to Brooklyn, I to the West Side.

I sleep fully. I wake rested.

Drinking feels like a game of Russian roulette.

And a new voice echoing in my head: "Are we having fun yet?"

On our second date, Clark drinks, I don't, we make out, and I think he's . . . fine? Making out on the sidewalk, he makes his blatant desire known and invites me to a third date of dinner at his place. I fake confirmations of enthusiasm back. But find myself entirely disinterested in seeing him again too.

Sobered in a new sense of the word, I see my situation clearly.

You might think, after fifty-plus *Love Bites* episodes exploring the intricacies of dating, I'd have a long list of needs in a partner. But studying humanity's complexity has helped me whittle to only three vital character traits: curiosity, passion, and goodness. If Curious, he'll seek to understand experiences outside his own and look to books, podcasts, newspapers, film, or music; he'll want to know as much about my mind as I'll want to know about his. If Passionate, he'll embrace his capabilities and curiosities, do more than "work to live," and support my passion for living. And if Good, he'll strive for kindness and compassion toward himself and others.

All other details are negotiable.

But alcohol tricks my mind into patching personality black holes in potential Mr. CPGs. It blurs lines and rose-colors my glasses. It highlights admirable qualities and softens my instinct screaming *no*. "Alcohol tends to put me on a kind of vixen autopilot in situations like that," writes Julia Bainbridge in an essay.[39] Recently, I've vixen autopiloted through a man who didn't ask me a single question about myself after hours together. One who didn't seek a cultural perspective outside his own. One who loved to touch my body but couldn't hold a candle to my mind. One who celebrated violence. One who turned dark after one too many polite rejections. One who just couldn't see me at all in his quest to show himself. "I know that's why I seized up when someone whose lips I wasn't so sure about letting touch mine advanced toward them," Julia then reflects of a sober date.

I decide: I will stop dating until I'm ready for you, Mr. CPG.

Because when things in my life are going well, I don't date men with hues of sexism, racism, machismo, and weakness hiding underneath the surface of only . . . fine. I don't obsess over numbers on a scale. I don't overanalyze my drinking. I don't kiss out of politeness. I don't wait for an excuse to exit.

When things are going well, I eat, drink, date, and move on.

And so when all is well within again, I'll see you clearly.

No matter what might be happening without.

SUGARFREE

PHYSICAL HEALTH: I'm nine pounds down and counting. I'm sleeping a little better. I don't want a drink. I don't want a brownie. I can't deny it; my body has changed. I began this Challenge confessing "every failed attempt scars against future hope" fears. But secretly, I *wanted* this Challenge to fail. Because if it succeeded, I knew I'd keep at it, losing another pleasure for the sake of my body. "At least sugar is easy to identify," Ben said in support. True. But it's hard to hear such advice from friends not contemplating indefinite loss. I don't know how long I'll keep this up. But I'm not hopping off the wagon just yet.

SOCIAL INTERACTIONS: Real friends don't stop liking you when you don't eat sugar or drink alcohol. Emma, Max, Rebecca, Polly, Emily, Erika, Meg, Janet, Paul, Vinay, Robbie, Abigail, Brent, Ben, and Deanna ate and drank with me during this Challenge. Some consumed things I couldn't, others let my abstinence give them an excuse not to drink. None guilted me for my choices. My family didn't either. We spent Thanksgiving with Nana in the rehab center where she was recouping from her fall. I made a pie I could not eat, slept on Nana's bed when too sick to stay awake, Lil' Sis drove me home in my car, and I was thankful. And men? Love *bites* right now. And I'm okay with that.

SENSE OF SELF: Dr. Kleifield once suggested my struggle with weight gain might be more correlated to mourning over my physical limitation than superficial angst; I exercise and eat robustly when healthy, and so being over- or underweight is my inability reflected back to me daily. Without "little indulgences" of brownies in bed or wine at work, nothing rose-colors this self-reflection either. The loneliness I thought conquered during the No Social Media Challenge? The fog obscuring why my life doesn't have momentum, clarity, or actionable joy? I now feel open wounds of anger, frustration, and despair.

***

In *Stumbling on Happiness*, psychologist and Harvard professor Daniel Gilbert defines *experience* versus *awareness*. He explains that the Latin origin of the word *experience* means "to try": experience is active. The Greek origin of the word *aware* means "to see": awareness is observational. "In fact, awareness can be thought of as a kind of experience of our own experience," Gilbert says.[40]

One hundred and sixty-eight days into this Year, I'm acutely observant.

Life without social media, shopping, and sugar have morphed into something more than a mere recording of individual parts— they've merged into a sum stage of something new and unexpected.

I'm experiencing my own experience.

I'm not sure what it means yet.

I'm not sure I like it.

Late on the final night of the Challenge, a wave of overwhelming panic hits. (They've been coming rather frequently of late.) As I lie in the darkness, the single-sick-broke burden crashes down in a rush of sweat-inducing, heart-palpitating anxiety. I'm paralyzed by fright until I think:

I can get my stashed brownies from the freezer!

I can make a martini or crack open a bottle of wine!

But I don't do any of those things.

I have to keep ripping off Band-Aids until absolutely sure I'm not the one keeping myself from the things I truly want.

At the end of this No Sugar Challenge, I feel no closer to *happy. period* days. But Gilbert says humans are horrible at conceptualizing time. We can easily visualize *space*—just shut your eyes and imagine a Frisbee flying toward your head. But because our brains compute sensory stimulation from the here and now, we imagine the future by visualizing pages flipping on a calendar or leaves coloring on trees. We have to see *now* change to *then*. "Because we naturally use our present feelings as a starting point when we attempt to predict our future feelings," Gilbert says, "we expect our future to feel a bit more like our present than it actually will."[41]

I cling to this concept like a lifeline.

Because almost halfway through my Year, I'm slimmer, sober, and standing with wounds gaping wide. This is all I know. All I feel.

Just in time for the ho-ho-holidays.

CHAPTER 4

NO HOLIDAY GIFTING

CHALLENGE: No Holiday Gifting/Consumerism

TIME LINE: Thanksgiving through the New Year

RULES: I will not give or receive holiday gifts. I will not buy any form of cheer (other than a fresh tree). Instead, I will share joy in word and deed.

OFFERING

Department stores liberated women and established Christmas tradition.

Well, they liberated *some* women and established the *commercialism* of Christmas gift-giving traditions.

Not that very long ago, women weren't readily welcome in public spaces. "A lady ought not to present herself alone in a library or museum, unless she goes there to study or work as an artist," advised one mid-nineteenth-century book on ladies' etiquette.[42] "Be not too often seen in public," warned another.[43] As such, not all restaurants welcomed women and restrooms were scarce, making a leisurely day in town not feasible. These made procuring goods at independent milliners, haberdashers, and dressmakers even more exhausting errands than the equivalent today.

That all began to change with the department store.

Starting in the 1850s, Macy's in New York City and Marshall Field's in Chicago offered upwardly middle-class women a new way to spend their days and dollars, bringing delights of all kinds under one massive roof. R. H. Macy's illuminated store windows fashioned the idea of "window shopping." He premiered in-store cafés where women could dine, tipple, *and* pee after![44] At Marshall Field's, partner Harry Gordon Selfridge introduced a reading room, a drop-off nursery, and ladies' facilities with onsite nurses. Goods traditionally protected in wooden closets were put on display to be touched and caressed, which encouraged browsing—a shocking concept in a time when social norms advised women to "not needlessly consume the time of the clerk and keep other customers waiting."[45] Shopping became social as well as socially acceptable.

"I came along just at the time when women wanted to step out on their own," Selfridge said. "They came to the store and realized some of their dreams."[46]

Until this time, Christmas was but a religious day for some. The Puritans didn't celebrate it. It wasn't an official federal holiday until 1870. Charles Dickens's Christmas stories planted seeds of lavish Victorian-era Christmases across the pond, and Macy and Selfridge sealed the deal in the US. Macy hired the first department store Santa Claus.[47] Selfridge first penned the phrase "Only [so many] days until Christmas."[48] Such marketing schemes built anticipation and established economic trends. As decades passed, more stores became theaters where anyone could create at home the holiday tableaus they saw on display.

Department stores founded a connection between Christmas and gifting.

Many of our earliest memories are grounded by the repetition of holidays: the same foods, services, clothes, and patterns of gift giving mark our growth from year to year. We may struggle against some inherited traditions as we grow, but we often repeat them as we establish our own families and adulthood holiday habits.

I grew up one of four children, as did my father. Through my childhood, his siblings rotated hosting Christmas Eve. We'd eat fish cakes, pork and clams, and the fried dough my avó— grandmother—let us stretch with our hands before she dropped them into bubbling oil and then tossed them, hot and crisp, in a bag with white sugar before guiding our very same ones back to us again. After midnight Mass, a relative dressed as Santa Claus would come bearing bags of presents from the extended family, including matching pajamas chosen by my mother for my sibling quartet. Buzzed on the company of cousins (and fried dough), we'd scramble into the car for the long drive home, then groggily climb into bed. Christmas Day would pass with the thrill of new toys, Nana and Poppa's ravioli, movies, and naps with the dog. I remember one Christmas of matching red flannel and the entire Ramona Quimby book series. Another, the marvel of receiving a Cabbage Patch doll *and* Pound Puppies. Every year, a new ornament Mom would date and pack into our designated boxes. Every year, we baked the same cookies, watched the same movies, sang the same songs together.

It all seemed made by magic.

Of course, now I know better.

Human hands produce the picture-perfect tableau. Planning and active, busy hands result in Santa visits, matching pajamas, roast dinner, and piped cookies. Nowadays, Pinterest boards and banner ads bring more ideas of "the perfect Christmas" into our view at every turn. But while we may start the season with lofty ambitions, reality often has us spending more time shopping for the perfect scene than living it.

Seeing joy in children's eyes at the final product can help make the finale feel worth the labor. But none in my sibling quartet has children yet. (*Please* don't mention this to my parents.) We've shifted some responsibility to share in the hosting, baking, and transporting. And we all buy gifts—for everyone—plus the stocking stuffers our parents used to handle on their own. This includes partners and any of their visiting relatives, godparents and godchildren, roommates, and any others at our holiday table. It's a lot of people with varying incomes and opinions about holiday gifting. Some enjoy it and feel it a fundamental part of Christmas tradition. Others feel overwhelmed and ready to simplify. We love one another fiercely. We struggle to find common ground. Every year, mounds of presents topple.

I love Christmas today even more than I did in childhood. I start my "so many days until Christmas" with holiday music in August. Roomie Erika put a kibosh on planning our holiday party until after Halloween. (November 1, I'm ready.) I stream the rom-com *Twelve Dates of Christmas* (you read that right) to keep my mind calm when I'm stress-cooking food-writer recipes or private chef gigs. I cherish the cheer of the season. I partake in hyperattentive thoughtfulness to the max.

But I don't find shopping an ideal social event even *before* mandated holiday gifting gets layered on. Driving, parking, looking, lifting, debating, interacting, buying, wrapping . . . the ritual can be exhausting. For those with illness and disability, there's then inaccessible parking, traversing large stores, fluorescent light, loud sound, no seating, impassible spaces . . . the ritual can be symptomatically triggering. Done en masse, gifting takes attention away from the holiday. On Christmas Eve, I'm wrapping instead of cooking with Dad or running out for last-minute gifts instead of visiting with my sisters during their limited time home. I cherish watching the Macy's Thanksgiving Day Parade with my family; I avoid the foot-traffic crush of shopping in Macy's at all costs. And if this Year's No Shopping Challenge taught me anything, I know the *stuff* I give won't definitely make anyone happy anyway.

"Would that Christmas could just be, without presents," bemoans my (fictional) fellow liberated thirty-something singleton Bridget Jones. "It is just so stupid, everyone exhausting themselves, miserably hemorrhaging money on pointless items nobody wants . . ."[49]

If there's a time for me to go without holiday gifting, it's this Year.

I e-mail my family that I would like to not give or receive gifts this Christmas. I justify that this will significantly contribute to my Without study: How will I feel when they open nothing from me or I sit empty-handed? What will fill my time in the absence of the hunt, the purchase, the wrap? I will not be allowed to make anything to gift: can I compensate in word and deed?

Their reactions vary, but they acquiesce.

Lil' Sis Maggie responds the most enthused: "We'll do *presence* instead."

I like that.

I take it one step further.

A few days before the No Shopping Challenge ended, I'd run into a discount department store for (needed) pet supplies. On display up front were hand towels with snowflakes and owls on them; a perfect no-reason present for Lizzie. I quickly lost time to perusing plates and Christmas candles, envisioning future decorating schemes. I realize now that this will snare me everywhere unless I rule out all forms of pageantry for purchase.

If department stores created the Christmas traditions that now bind me, I'll remove myself from them entirely.

This holiday I'll not buy *any* commercial form of cheer.

"First thing tomorrow. Good plan," Bridget Jones cheers in my head.

I feel more liberated already.

THANKSGIVING

I'm making my Thanksgiving pie when I hear a familiar voice squeak out from the television in the living room. I race in to see a friend from past theater days dressed in full elf garb, popping up alongside shoppers in a department store, the spokesperson for their holiday campaign. Her bright red hair and perky smile instantly bring a grin to my face. I laugh, watching her.

The Hershey Kisses Christmas commercial follows. It's played every year since 1989,[50] but I never grasped how much I look forward to hearing it "for the first time this Christmas" until now. Tears prickle as the animated chocolates, like handbells, ring "We Wish You a Merry Christmas." Nostalgia spreads warmth through my chest as the final chocolate bell wipes his brow with his paper plume, relieved in his musical success.

I, too, feel relief.

I've been worried that not buying gifts might, indeed, lower the emotional significance of this season. But standing in a flour-covered apron with tears streaming, I recognize that traditions and the joy of surprise will move me in the moment because I genuinely love Christmas.

Lil' Sis is right. I don't need *presents*. I have *presence*.

I look at my calendar threads to note upcoming holiday events.

Roomie Erika and I host a monthly "Riverside Writers" group; this month partners will join for a holiday dinner I'll cook after our meeting. We have those tickets to the two holiday shows bought back during the No Shopping Challenge. One of my skinny-Sell neighbors is a Ballerina in the New York City Ballet, and usually passes me free last-minute tickets to their Nutcracker every year; I send out a wish that manifests. I'm excited for Sweet Friend Lisa's midmonth cookie exchange party. On Christmas Eve, I'll go early to Nana and Poppa's to cook dinner for my family. Christmas Day will be at Dad's. The rest of this Challenge I'll let come, moment by moment!

Moving through the holidays, my Christmas playlist fills the air. Roomie Erika and I lovingly select our fresh tree (the one caveat to the rules), then goofily carry it up Broadway like Harry and Sally. We take refuge from the cold in theaters and marvel at bodies dancing to Christmassy tunes. Our Riverside Writers dinner table dazzles in red and gold as we clink vintage crystal stemware and devour good food. My Ballerina comes through with Nutcracker tickets, and I shed tears of awe at her onstage power and grace. At the cookie party, I catch up with Sweet Friend Lisa and meet new people. In Connecticut during a snowstorm, I light a fire and work beside its warmth as snow falls. I watch through *It's a Wonderful Life*, *Home Alone*, *Rare Exports*, *Emmet Otter's Jug Band Christmas*, *Scrooged* . . . I pass store windows, surprised by the absence of urge to buy.

All goes according to plan.

But December 19, something's troubling me.

I pace Riverside Drive, trying to identify what feels *off*. It's nothing akin to the crave for a Twitter or Amazon hit, nor a hangry wail like that for a cocktail. Not giving gifts doesn't stand me crying in the shower . . . No. But some new cloud has permeated this Challenge. Mitra and I walk and walk, waiting for my thoughts to clear. (Which they do more easily now, as I give them time.)

We turn a corner.

They open.

It all feels *flat*.

At the Writers dinner, Erika chatted at the table while I largely hid in the kitchen, cooking and cleaning. When finally seated, sipping bubbly water instead of bubbly wine, I faded into the glow of tree lights rather than participate in the jolly tableau my hands had created. I baked my Ballerina a thank-you gift of pirouette-fueling low-sugar, high-protein cookies (an un-Christmassy gift within rules); for Sweet Friend Lisa's cookie exchange the next day, instead of making sugar-capped snowflakes, gingerbread men, chocolate-kissed krinkles, or any of the other dozens upon dozens in my repertoire, I just brought the second half of that batch. There, I also stayed sober, keeping conversation light and impersonal. I left early, planning to stop at the Rockefeller Tree. But instead I . . . went home.

I am doing the traditions.

I feel calm. Thankful.

But no genuine moments of joy fuel me.

With one week until Christmas, how will I swap purchase for purpose?

Am I waiting for a Christmas miracle?

Or do I just think I *should* miss the feeling of Christmas?

I take to the Internet for advice. *The New York Times* column "Room for Debate" positions scholars from various backgrounds. I find one tackling the question: "Why aren't people happier during the holidays?"[51]

Neuroscientist Matthew Lieberman hypothesizes our "amazing knack for imagining and comparing" dooms us to failure, as those picture-perfect tableaus and Dickensian Christmas stories set unrealistic expectations. He recommends to "stop comparing your life to the Cleavers and consider what your life would be like if your friends and loved ones were gone from it. Although it might be sad to consider, it also reminds us of the ways in which we are blessed." No one has to tell me how lucky I am in my loved ones; this lack of cheer isn't from want of blessings. But counting them doesn't seem to get me anywhere.

Psychologist and researcher Sonja Lyubomirsky theorizes that increased holiday work doesn't make the payoff worth it. Researchers have found that everyday annoyances can be harder on us than calamities and that daily delights have a bigger impact on our well-being more than major events," she says. She suggests we simplify holiday chores so to save energy and leave space for the thrill of daily surprise. At my dinner party, I used chores as an excuse to hide from interacting with the Writers—cleaning wasn't a stress that delayed me. Otherwise, this Challenge is all about reduction and presence. Still, no magic.

Economist Andrew J. Oswald says holiday highs and lows statistically cancel out: "Evidence suggests that people are not much happier in the holiday season than at other times." Some "painstaking statistical" studies show a drop in self-harm during the holidays; others, an increase in emergency room arrivals, inferred from an increase in alcohol consumption and traffic injuries. He concurs that success in holiday happiness resides in diminishing high expectations and limiting actions so to then savor present moments. (And to watch booze intake.)

I read nonscholastic articles and listen to podcast episodes. Over and over, I find the same advice: if wanting but not feeling Christmas cheer, we should seek out nostalgia. We should turn on the music, watch the movies, and drive to the lights. We should trim the tree, make the food, find the friends, and volunteer the time. I see "best of" lineups. I see fill-in-the-blank lists. We're encouraged to *want* Christmassy. Then given ways to do, do, *do* until we feel it.

I sit with all of these and . . .

No.

Cocoa and carols don't repair a suffering body.

They don't fill an empty bank account.

They don't deliver a needed job.

Baking cookies won't bring back a lost loved one.

Or heal a broken heart.

We shouldn't have to fake feeling just because it's Christmas.

I make an active choice: I'll let this Christmas go.

On this exact midpoint in my Year's journey, I forgive myself for not compensating gifting with doing. Instead of filling time with rituals that would be superficial at best, I'll instead work through the inner layers of troubles exposed by these culminating explorations of *without*.

It hurts, this letting go.

But it's just one Christmas.

Maybe by next year, things will be different.

ACCOMMODATE

Stranger Than Fiction is not a Christmas movie.

And I didn't watch it this December.

But it's relevant to the week before Christmas.

(Warning: spoiler alerts ahead.)

In this quietly fascinating film, Emma Thompson plays Karen Eiffel, a novelist notorious for killing off her heroes in satisfying deaths of staggering genius. We meet her at the height of emotional angst: she doesn't know how Harold Crick should die. With her voice narrating, we see Harold (Will Ferrell) and follow the mundane motions that fill his days: his patterns of hygiene, his routine work as a tax auditor, his lack of interpersonal relationships. Of course, Harold doesn't know he is a character being drafted in the pages of a novel. That is, not until we witness the first moment he hears Karen's narration; the very moment Harold Crick the person merges with Harold Crick the character. But Karen isn't aware she's writing, page by page, the life of a real human being. In the quiet gaps of time during which she envisions options for what she believes his fictional impending death, Harold searches for his nonfictional novelist, hoping to alter the genre.

Finally, we move toward the moment when the two come together! Karen writes—the phone rings—and hers does! We see her confusion! Her fear! Petrified, she types once more—it rings again—and it's Harold Crick on the other end! The moment comes! Character and author first speak!

And so, dear human! Now begins such an adventure for me . . .

. . . and me.

My Dear Friend Rebecca thinks My Year, Without ripe for penning. She recently mentioned it to a literary agent who I then met, liked, and signed with. Now, I'm to spend the holidays outlining a book proposal and writing a No Sugar chapter sample. (I vow to not let this affect the project; nothing is more important.) And so, with only a few days left until Christmas and me still no elf, I pore over blog posts and journals, taking a Karen Eiffel look at the Harold Crick I play in the story of my life.

Winter slams the East Coast. I'm sicker than ever. Movement softens some kinds of pain but agitates others. Medication takes off only the worst edge. I work propped up in bed, a table alongside filled with chargers, notes, pens, tea, and bottles.

I dig into journals.

I see RoboWriter.

Late November, I'd noticed myself checking his Twitter feed too many times and so took a week off from social media to reset again. I don't quite understand the pull—I hardly knew the guy—and so now try to sleuth it out in my scribbles. Do feelings only linger because he was the most recent paramour? Is the mild cyberstalking merely bruised ego because he ended it? What dulled my "spark" to the point that he felt none in the end? I distinctly remember him pulling away from our first kiss and saying "wow" when I pulled away and said "meh" (to myself in my head because I'm not an asshole).

I trace a path back to that *Love Bites* episode with Tarot Sasha, before I was to meet RoboWriter for dinner. Her advice to armor myself like the Knight of Swords helped me stay strong, calm, and present through to the end. Robo had complimented my vigor through illness and my capability to excel in a field hard even for those without physical burden. But reading back, I also don't see any invitation to expose my pain. I see good reason to not risk vulnerability. Not to take off the armor.

I think to the guy just before him. He made me laugh, and we'd talk animatedly for hours about literature and life, and I wouldn't admit to myself how much he lacked in emotional generosity. We dated for several months until he voiced concern about my physical limitation.

The guy from the porch was soft and sensitive, but it wasn't long before I worried he wasn't making space for me far beyond bed and table and realized I was but a postdivorce refresh.

Before him was the friend who became a lover while we both reeled from broken hearts. Just as I started wanting something real, he told me he was healed and ready to date again. A year later, he shared that our relationship helped him realize how greatly he wanted to be a father. A lovely compliment. (I can't have children.)

Before him, another.

Around them, others.

And before all of them, Ruark.

I rise from working in bed and take down for my tea the snowman mug his aunt gave me so many Christmases ago. (It was once part of a set; does he still own the other?) Ruark lives in an incontestable part of my heart, but I've never regretted our shift to friendship. Having observed the beautiful tableau of his wife and kids, I know he hasn't either. But I ponder his family that once felt like mine. Did any part of them consider me "less than" because I couldn't give him children too?

This all starts an ache.

As Karen Eiffel, I choose what you see of the path I've recorded.

But this story is not fiction.

And here, the phone rings.

Because this Christmas, I spend time studying journals and shaping Challenge into Chapter. Thoughts and feelings arise perhaps not brought back to light otherwise. This Christmas, I comprehend and brood again over how I am so very much alone.

"We are all alone," says Julia Bainbridge.

Julia's the "vixen autopilot" essayist. Like me, she also writes about food and culture. She's also in her midthirties. And she also struggles with loneliness. But Julia does not have a chronic illness and Julia does host *The Lonely Hour* podcast, which explores loneliness and solitude in modern society. I figure no better person can funhouse mirror my quandary.

On *The Lonely Hour*, loneliness is not an emotion to be feared. Rather, Julia approaches loneliness as merely one in "the mixed bag of emotions involved in the human experience," she describes to me of breaking the stigma. She speaks with those who experience unique kinds of voluntary or involuntary solitude, asking what they learned from loneliness felt during that time.

We first try to articulate what our versions of rock-bottom loneliness feel like but can't single it out. It often mingles with depression. It can show when making significant life decisions while single, then fade again. As such, we struggle to define chronic loneliness too; time shared in a romantic context doesn't guarantee dispelled loneliness. "Even if I get into 'that relationship' I still will be inherently alone, as we all are," Julia ponders. "I think there are times throughout the course of life when that hits a little harder and you feel lonely over it."

It was once assumed the loneliest among us are those who live alone or at the outer reaches of society. But an abundance of research has proven this wrong. Julia calls neuroscientist and psychologist John Y. Cacioppo a "rock star" of the loneliness field. Cacioppo defines loneliness as "perceived social isolation"[52] and "a complex set of feelings encompassing reactions to unfulfilled intimate and social needs."[53] Loneliness is a perception, not a circumstance. It's defined by how we *feel* in regard to those around us.

In one survey of 2,632 male and female Ohio State University students—those at peak age and place of social interaction— Cacioppo discovered professed loneliness across majors and despite varying hours of study. Roommate situations provided no indication of whether or not someone would feel lonely. Nor did participation or absence in campus organizations. Health or exercise markers played no part.

Anyone could feel socially isolated. Anyone could feel lonely.

Cacioppo and his team then conducted an intensive neurological study of the most controlled median of that group. Compared to nonlonely peers, these students had lower autonomic reactions (heart rate and activity) when mimicking asking someone for a date, doing arithmetic, or listing mundane daily activities. Across both social and nonsocial tasks, "cardiovascular reactivity tended to be the lowest for the lonely individuals. These data are consistent with the notion that lonely individuals are emotionally withdrawn," the report concludes.[54] The students had greater problems falling asleep, staying asleep, and falling into restorative REM cycle. They released more salivary cortisol (stress hormones) throughout the day and particularly during the evenings, when structured social class time ended and solitude increased.

Surprisingly to me, these lonely kids did not seek comfort in drugs or alcohol; socially embedded students drink more than lonely kids. But in regard to what I've learned about how stress and sleep affect our long-term health, I can only imagine the cumulative damage on young bodies. If their loneliness goes unchanged, I worry what comfort they might seek after college ends.

A recent study of 2,861 adults in the Netherlands, ages forty to seventy-five, explored how perceived isolation affects the odds of developing type 2 diabetes mellitus (T2DM).[55] Those with healthy glucose levels, prediabetes, newly diagnosed T2DM, and established T2DM were surveyed. Loneliness was quantified by a long list of factors: the individual's number of family members and close acquaintances, the emotional and practical support found in those relationships, time spent interacting socially overall, etc. When graphing results, practicalities including cohabitation, physical isolation, and frequency of contact were compared against glucose levels. Across the board, those deemed lonely were at greater risk for prediabetes or had been newly diagnosed. For each 10 percent drop in network friendships, the odds of a woman (specifically) already having T2DM increased 14 percent! Living alone didn't increase odds for women (it did exponentially for men). But a lack of social participation was a strong indicator.

The study didn't attempt to explain why this happens; it merely tracked that it does. But thinking back to what Dr. B and Taubes taught me in the No Sugar Challenge, I wonder if it has something to do with insulin—that pesky master controlling hormone—and how it intertwines with glucose and stress hormones?

Could loneliness be a factor in my blood sugar struggle too?

A more recent Cacioppo *et al.* study on the neurology of loneliness warns that *chronic* loneliness puts the body in continuous self-preservation mode; solo people have to constantly provide for and defend themselves and, with no one to take over the watch, must therefore stay in elevated fight-or-flight. Over time, this increases distrust in others, decreases an ability to feel pleasure when socializing, and reduces an ability to take risks.[56]

Julia and I discuss testing bias and limitations in these studies and how many who are most in need of assistance are often not included in test populations. We look to these statistics as points for discussion, more than answers. But across the board, science and psychology concur that feeling lonely isn't exactly healthy.

And here I am: lonely and getting sicker.

But even in our present states of loneliness, Julia and I both recognize strong social networks. "I have deep friendships despite those people having seen me in pretty unattractive situations," she shares. Such invested friends help weigh out big decisions and provide comfort if we chose wrong. "But at the end of the day, I'm still alone," she again resolves.

"Have you always felt that way?"

"Yes."

"Okay."

"It's confirmed the more I talk to people . . . We are individual human beings with brains that are our own. We may choose to share our deepest, darkest thoughts. But as there are things we always edit out, they're still our own. A lot of the problems we face are ours to surmount. Other people can be leaned on and help. But at the end of the day, you are you, and the problems you face are yours, and it's up to you to fix them. Or not."

I counter that others would say we are *not* alone. Cacioppo points out that "evolution has sculptured the human genome to be sensitive to and succoring of contact and relationships with others," and a need to communicate is vital and universal across cultures.[5]

"I guess I'd say both are true," she concludes.

I guess I'd agree.

But these questions—what is being alone and what is loneliness—hang over my Christmastime. I worry if loneliness plays into the decisions I make: Do I subconsciously doubt others? Does my desperation for companionship, paying work, and better health underscore my interactions? Has loneliness altered my ability to collaborate? What fault is mine for these men in my past starting strong with their affection but then fading fast?

I ask Julia how podcast guests have taken action after identifying loneliness. She shares how one recognized that jealousy over her sister's newborn son was encouraging self-flagellating, bitter thoughts over her own childlessness; the recognition inspired her to make moves and choose single motherhood through sperm donor insemination. After articulating his isolated reality on *The Lonely Hour*, another accepted that he'd given his life in Belgium all he could and moved to London; he now lives happily among friends and is engaged.

"Most people who aren't chronically lonely, and thus handicapped to the point where they can't move out of it, do move out of it. They sort of get over themselves, in a way," Julia points out. "I mean, don't you ever feel that? When you've talked about your problems with a bunch of different friends and you're like, 'I'm so sick of talking about myself' or 'I'm sick of the feeling'—I'm sick of *whatever*. It just sort of ends, at a certain point."

We agree: it can be as simple as deciding to move forward.

Despite the risks Cacioppo's latter study warns (we're also younger than that studied demographic), Julia's loneliness doesn't prevent her from making big moves or taking risks; she's never had a problem jumping feet first into a new world. "I should probably think more before I do, in general," she says. I don't know where I stand on that line anymore. I used to feel brave, changing jobs and ZIP codes and using the word *boyfriend* as soon as I felt like it. Now, that dampened, indefinable *it*—"my juju, my life force, *whatever*"—remains a mystery.

Could this be chronic loneliness?

A Karen Eiffel with life-or-death questions unanswered, days pass. And now, Christmas Eve morning.

I find myself lazy and delaying. I'm not worried—I'll make it to my grandparents' with plenty of time to cook. I enjoy my coffee and luxuriate in the quiet hush that comes over Manhattan these few hours every year. Few cabs idle on Riverside Drive. No machines dig into concrete. No one slams on a horn. All is muted; languid.

For the first time in my adult life, I pack not a single present into the car. I cram in no platters of cookies, ceremonial bottles of wine, or bouquets of flowers. This feels against my nature; both sides of my family have raised me to never walk into a house empty-handed. I worry I won't be enough on my own. But as I buckle Mitra in and warm up the engine, the tinge of mourning makes way to a new kind of thrill: I have hours ahead to cook with my grandparents and two days without anticipating a material reward. Just family, stories, and hugs.

Up the West Side Highway, over the Hudson, and into Connecticut we fly, no traffic to delay us. All is mild and warm and green. My heart feels lighter than it has in days. I acknowledge my solitude but quickly let the sensitivity around it go. This is my Christmas *without*, and I'll relish the drive!

I sing to cheesy radio music!

I crack the windows and breathe fresh air!

It's Christmas Eve, and all is well!

Halfway into the journey, one of the exes calls.

"Merry Christmas!"

"Merry Christmas!" I sing back.

"I got married two weeks ago!"

I feel my face pale.

"Congratulations!"

His voice now sounds garbled in my ear as he updates me on it all. How the event was both planned and unplanned, a way to "make it official," and they're celebrating a quiet Christmas with friends. I hear my voice reply how *happy* I am for their happiness! I hear the smile in his voice—*so happy!*—as he updates me on his work, his creative plans for the New Year. He asks about the radio show. I prattle about a new series we're launching. He asks about this Year. I ramble about signing with the agent. I do feel genuine joy for him. But a part of my heart is crumbling, just a little.

"Merry Christmas!" once again.

We hang up.

He was the beau who wants children I can't give.

I use this as an excuse for why he ended things.

But I know, I just wasn't *her*. He married *her*.

All is calm. All is bright . . . right?

I drive.

My brain turns back to all those men I dated . . .

All those good men in transitions or rough places . . .

All those men for whom sparks flew and then fell . . .

All those men whose egos and dicks I fluffed back to attention . . .

All those men who needed me and then *did not need me* . . .

The men who then so easily hugged goodbye and walked away . . .

The men who were then ready to find *her* soon after?

My heart **howls** out to the empty parkway!

Am I always to breathe low while men unpack baggage at my feet? Am I to suffer their jealousies but not deserve their commitment? Am I to desperately overcompensate for what my body cannot do— not absence of action but the result of a *fucking bug that bit me over twenty years ago*—only to be judged by men who can't grow up from any emotional quibble on their own? Am I to accommodate every personality quirk just to—as Julia put it—get "exasperated dating all these fuck boys" afterward? Do I not deserve a cheery drive home for Christmas without an ex's fulfilled quest for partnership thrown in my face like some soured holiday pie?

I go to their weddings!

I welcome their spouses and babies!

I support their happy. fucking. period unions!

But *where are you*?!

Do I never get to meet my Mr. CPG?

I'm lost to anguish when my friend Marcia texts: "Merry Christmas!"

Via Siri, I respond: "EX MARRIED FREAKING." "Do you have *Queens Greatest Hits* in the car?" I don't. She sends YouTube links. (And then stops texting, because I'm driving and she's a smart friend.) I hit PLAY. "Find Me Somebody to Love" blasts through Lil' Blue and I scream-sing out a desperate prayer. I pound out on the steering wheel to the beat of "Fat Bottomed Girls." I shimmy my shoulders to "Under Pressure."

I'm crying?

No. I'm laughing!

I thank the empty highway for Marcia!

I thank the trees for Christmas!

I thank the clouds for being homeward bound!

I am a force to be reckoned with again!

And I am not alone with my screaming soul.

Julia started *The Lonely Hour* to explore stories of isolation, yes. But also because she "would be at parties in New York, looking around at these thoroughbred women who were the same age, ready for partnership, ambitious, successful, well-presented, and attractive—women whose doors should be beaten down by suitors—all looking around, like . . . Where are they?" Yes, it ends up *The Lonely Hour* does a damned good job of funhouse mirroring my isolation. But she also provides (bittersweet) comfort in that I am only one among many queens carving her own path.

Queens . . . ?

Yes.

This word—triggered by Marcia's music choice—starts something.

Because Julia's right. Sometimes you just get over yourself.

And it's time to get right with myself.

I don't know how yet, but this habit loop of negative thought stops here.

Right now, I'm gonna drive home for Christmas.

But no narrator or neurological study is killing off this character.

Come January, this Harold Crick is taking back her story.

EXCHANGE

PHYSICAL BODY: In the absence of holiday shopping, I saved myself the additional stress Lyubomirsky warns leaves us too busy for genuine moments of daily joy. This also saved me from further sickening my already sick body. I would have loved to *do* more this holiday. But in the grand scheme of things, I'll take this as an incidental gift.

SOCIAL INTERACTIONS: No denouncement came for my not gifting or overcompensating in deed. No one called me Grinch or Scrooge. Everyone in my life seems a bit *tired* this year. Time together was time well appreciated.

SENSE OF SELF: This is the first time in adulthood I've given myself permission to not give. Communicating that choice was the hardest part. It feels somewhat selfish; I didn't end this Challenge with any practical to-do lists of how to give aside from gifting. But I have faith that lesson is still coming. "It's just one Christmas."

***

Charles Dickens wrote A *Christmas Carol* over six intense weeks in the fall of 1843. He apparently used no notes, nor drew outlines. We instead see direct revision on a sixty-six-page first draft. Six thousand printed copies with colorful illustrations by John Leech bound in red leather appeared in bookshops that December 19. By Christmas Eve, all had sold out.

Seeing himself in the miserly, wealthy, selfish Scrooge, one notable American industrialist gave his employees an extra day off.[58] In his literary journal, the poet Thomas Cook reviewed it as a "blessed inspiration." Of Scrooge's redemption, Cook asked readers to question "whether we have not grown *Scroogey?*"[59] A beloved holiday story still, it's a question that often begs for reflection every December the 24th.

Finally home for Christmas, I wouldn't say I feel particularly Scroogey; just like I'd thrilled in childhood when Avó returned the magical pastry to my hands, so my heart lifts cooking at Poppa's side. As we set lamb to roast and chop vegetables, I ask about his holiday memories. What was his mother like? Did he get along with his father? Was he closest with one particular sibling? As he talks, I see the child in my ninety-year-old grandfather. We eat in a living room overheated to keep Nana's healing body in extra comfort. I watch my family open presents, feeling neither jealousy for my empty hands nor disgust for their full ones. Gratitude for today is the only gift I need this Year.

And then Mom hands me a card.

My dearest Jacqueline,

This has been a very hard Christmas – made even harder because I had to respect your wishes for no gifts. How hard it was to not get your pj's!! But I know good things are coming. We have each other. Lots of love and family are what's important. I am so looking forward to our movie nights in my (our!) new home.

Always, with lots of love, hugs, and kisses,
Mom

My throat closes.

I had anticipated such complications in this particular Challenge.

To one person, mandated gifting can feel a stressful act put upon by habitual commercialism and Selfridge-esque marketing schemes. To another, it is a true act of love, genuine in intent and purpose. In her sacrifice, my mother loves me with unselfish generosity. Her card references our family's year of illness and accident, business failure and job conflict. She's moved into a new house but, devoting time to my grandparents, not yet unpacked. She's offered it as home to me, too, if my condition gets worse. I joke we'll Grey Gardens it together until that image makes us blanch, and we shift the daydream to *Gilmore Girls*. In the absence of a gift to give, I make a vow: next year, I'll make sure she celebrates joyfully in her new home.

On Christmas Day, I passively observe the gift exchange at Dad's too. We eat, we talk, and we play games. Laughter mingles with tears. It's a muted Christmas. We're tired. We're hopeful. We're together. We hug tightly before separating to bedrooms or homes for the night.

Big Sis and I settle on to the couch to watch *The Muppet Christmas Carol*. A glorious adaptation of Dickens's classic, it never fails to make my heart fly. Sis sits behind me, I lay my head in her lap, and she presses her fingers against my forehead and across my temples; my body so sore and tired, I melt in the comfort. I rouse to sing with the Muppets—we know this story well—but fall asleep before Scrooge professes his final "God bless us, every one!"

I wake up a little sad and a little lonely.

But I have Mom's hope to cling to:

"I know good things are coming."

CHAPTER
CHALLENGE **5**

NO NEGATIVE THOUGHT

CHALLENGE: No Negative Thought

TIME LINE: One month (thirty-one days)

RULES: Every time I catch myself in the habit of falling lost to a negative thought, I will cut it off, observe it, and change the dialogue around it.

FIXATION

It comes almost every night now.

I'm nearly dropped into dreamland when my brain catches on a thought. It's only a small one, like a grain of sand. And it seems far away, like on a mountain somewhere lost to shadow. It's but an echo of a thought, really.

It's enough.

I *don't have a deadline tomorrow.* My heart thumps.

The grain catches another.

I *don't have anything due next week either.* My breath quickens.

Do I have enough work to pay my bills? I don't! The air feels thick.
I'll never have enough work. My eyes shoot open wide.
I am alone. I am sick. I will always be alone. I will always be sick.

Now, I'm fully awake, panicked, gasping in the middle of a sandstorm.

I lie for hours, suffering, until my body gives in, and I sleep.

Then, there was that psychological question of my crying in the shower.

Then, that confusing contemplation on loneliness.

Then, that Christmas drive.

I have to get a handle on my ~~thoughts~~ ~~emotions~~ brain.

This habit of letting thoughts spiral into a black hole of grief.

For much of recorded human history, emotion has been considered a natural reaction to the physical world and separate from unique thought. Greek philosophy and cognitive psychology would have us believe our brains are wired by human evolution:[60] a trigger crosses our path, a certain part of the brain alights, then we *feel* and physically react in a predetermined way. As Meg Ryan so succinctly sums up when yelling at Kevin Kline in the movie *French Kiss*: "Happy, smile! Sad, frown! Use the corresponding face for the corresponding emotion!"

"This classical view of emotion is simple and intuitive,"[61] concludes Dr. Lisa Feldman Barrett, a psychologist, researcher, and university distinguished professor with over two hundred peer-reviewed papers on emotion in the brain. But Barrett hasn't found proof that it's true. Instead, she says "emotions are whole-brain affairs." Our one brain continually processes internal sensations—our metabolism, oxygen, blood pressure, blood sugar, etc.—as well as external stimuli and every memory we create. "Happiness, surprise, anger, and the rest are constructed in the moment by general-purpose systems throughout the brain, the same systems that create thoughts, memories, sights, sounds, smells, and other mental phenomena," Barrett explains. In a quick moment of *feeling*, our brain can only make a snap judgment about what that feeling might mean.

Living with illness, I already know this.

Back on that summer porch day when waves of horrible sensation coursed, I immediately ran a checklist of potential causes. Was it my blood sugar? Where might my estrogen level be? Was I under increased stress? I concluded symptoms of illness, not emotion. Conversely, I understand my nightly panic attacks are a physical reaction to thoughts of loneliness and fear; I connect my thumping heart and racing breath with the thoughts in my head, and as such I can describe that story in that specific way. On television, we often see the opposite: someone experiences those same chest-caving sensations and rushes to the hospital assuming a heart attack, only to be taught that a panic attack produces the same effect.

Without comprehension, our brain misconstrues what we feel.

Through clinical studies, Barrett and her colleagues have found that those who are better at identifying and verbally articulating their negative emotions also have more coping mechanisms in which to process them. These people may articulate more intense negative emotion than others, but they experience negative emotion less frequently overall because of this heightened ability to pick a tool, process the emotion, and move on from it.[62]

I started this Year in an *indefinable* fog. I couldn't describe the *it* that had left—"my juju, my life force, *whatever*." I keep looping back to even more painful variations on this loneliness theme. I need to better define these emotions and craft more tools so that I can move beyond the sandstorm once and for all.

I'm ready to take action.

But where do I start?

I think to the B*ust* article: why was it so easy for me to empathize with others suffering from the same self-esteem issues I still can't shake? I think to my work: why do I feel the need to hide behind interviews? To relationships: why do I compensate for my illness with so much patience that I then help romantic partners break things off with me?

Why can't I treat myself with as much kindness as I extend to others?

I bring this conundrum to Professor David, as many of his studies center on the correlation between compassion and self-control. "You beat yourself up because your mind is focused on saying what you should be doing—you're not seeing yourself as somebody else," he says. Without realizing it, our thoughts often trap us in internal monologue. Just like a computer screen blocks the social cues that warn us to "put the brakes on hurting people," we don't see the negative effect of only projecting out. Inside our mind, we often speak far more harshly to ourselves than we would to another in dialogue. "Imagine yourself as a real person with feelings," Professor David suggests. "Not just as the condemner, but also the person who is going to feel and hear and internalize that message."

For this Challenge, I will no longer be my condemner.

Every time I catch a grain of negative thought, I'll first shut it down. Then, I'll observe and define it just as I do the symptoms of my illness. I'll shift the harsh inner monologue to a kinder dialogue. And if my voice isn't a loving part of the conversation, I'll curate the voices in my head and use them to my advantage.

FW Lyndsey recently sent me a link to social psychologist Amy Cuddy's TED Talk, "Your Body Language May Shape Who You Are."

Cuddy concludes that when we feel small and powerless, we close our bodies and cower. Conversely, expressions of power show in broadened chests and stances that take up space. She claims popping into such expanded "power poses" increases confidence. I haven't looked into the validity of this yet. But one of Cuddy's poses looks like Wonder Woman, and she's an Amazon queen I wouldn't mind working into this conversation.

Then, there's Princess Leia.

Or more specifically, Carrie Fisher, the actress who played her.

Who died two days after Christmas.

Years ago, I'd listened to Fisher narrate the audiobook version of her one-woman play, Wishful Drinking. I appreciated how she brashly called out demons from her childhood of "Hollywood in-breeding" and Leia stardom at nineteen. She then laid bare, without apology and with wry humor, her adult struggles with addiction and mental illness. Life is hard. I admire those who so live with their tits out in defiance and celebration.

Her mother, the iconic film star Debbie Reynolds, passed the next day.

A 2010 story Reynolds shared on NPR also stuck with me. Cast at seventeen in Singin' in the Rain, she had no prior dance experience compared to costars Fred Astaire and Gene Kelly. Grueling rehearsals left her bruised, exhausted, and sore. One day, Astaire found her crying under a piano, ready to quit. He invited her to watch him rehearse, then danced until red in the face. She sat mesmerized and took with her that "even the greats find it hard to be really excellent. But you have to keep striving."[63]

For this Challenge, I'll shut down this habit of spiraling negative thought and then call upon the power of such badass women to lift me up. I'll think of Debbie Reynolds dancing "Good Morning" like it was no big thing. And Leia, who showed girls that princesses can grow up to be generals. I'll think of FW Lyndsey and Marcia and my mother and other women—other Wonder Women—who I know stand strong behind me.

This is a messy something.

But I can start with something.

Carrie Fisher once said:

"Sometimes you can only find heaven by slowly backing away from hell."[64]

In this Challenge, I welcome my hellish thoughts.

Because I'm ready to overthrow them.

RESISTANCE

Around ten o'clock, the night before this Challenge officially starts, I'm almost asleep when a grain catches and builds. Thoughts threaten to overwhelm. But then . . . I recognize I'm thinking them. Can I command panic to cease?

I try a simple word—*stop*.

I stare at the ceiling, unsure of what to do next.

I think of Wonder Women, and five names come in a flash.

Wonder Woman, Carrie Fisher, Michelle Obama, Lyndsey Ellis, Mitra.

I don't question them. I repeat their names over and over.

Wonder Woman, Carrie Fisher, Michelle Obama, Lyndsey Ellis, Mitra. Wonder Woman, Carrie Fisher, Michelle Obama, Lyndsey Ellis, Mitra. Wonder Woman, Carrie Fisher, Michelle Obama, Lyndsey Ellis, Mitra. Wonder Woman, Carrie Fisher, Michelle Obama, Lyndsey Ellis, Mitra. I repeat and repeat and repeat and find myself woozy. I fall back to sleep.

I wake again around eleven thirty, snapping to attention as if I'd never dozed. But this time, I immediately identify that I feel afraid, powerless, and disgusted with myself for being so. *Wonder Woman, Carrie Fisher, Michelle Obama, Lyndsey Ellis, Mitra. Wonder Woman, Carrie Fisher, Michelle Obama, Lyndsey Ellis, Mitra* . . .

I fall asleep for real this time.

The next morning, while coffee perks, I try a power pose.

I set the microwave timer for two minutes and face my broad kitchen windows. Following Cuddy's instructions, I plant my feet slightly wider than hip distance. I put my hands on my hips and spread my elbows. My shoulders fall, and my chest broadens. My heart starts to race uncomfortably, with my chest thrust so far forward; I shut my eyes and send my breath lower in my body to calm the chase. I focus on feeling my feet firmly planted on the cold linoleum. A new mantra comes: *My morning, my city, my day; my project, my work, my words.* I repeat these in my mind as I breathe in and out, words moving with inhalations and exhalations. *My morning, my city, my day; my project, my work, my words.* My heart races, but I feel strong, breathing and repeating. The timer rings. I pour coffee. I sit and work. I learn that two minutes of intention is two minutes of choosing the path I walk.

The next morning, Wonder Woman at the window only gets me so far.

I quickly find myself in an unexpected verbal altercation with a friend; the kind of nonfight you don't notice you're having until you sit down dazed, damaged, and unsure of how you were even hit. I spend the day reliving the rift, worrying about who was more in the wrong or what the friend might be thinking, and am far behind on work by nightfall. Dark thoughts combine: disappointment in myself, anger at her, disgust in us both. I start to spiral when I catch myself and: *Wonder Woman, Carrie Fisher, Michelle Obama, Lyndsey Ellis, Mitra. Wonder Woman, Carrie Fisher* . . .

"Fuck her!"

I snort-laugh!

Carrie Fisher in my head: "Why do you care so much what she thinks?"

Wait. What now?

I stop and assess.

I've been agonizing over "she said/I said" because I care about this human. And that's swell—I *like* being someone who invests emotionally in others, and it's important to value the decade of friendship we share. But being *so* open, vulnerable, and sympathetic that I can't put this relatively small altercation aside to prioritize my work for the present?

No. I don't like that.

I realize my mind has created another habit without my realizing: It easily helter-skelters when triggered by an emotional skirmish, flailing my pressing needs with it. In meditation—whether from Hindu or Buddhist or hippie-love-yoga teachers—we're taught that we can master our thoughts. I have little problem doing this when sitting in front of my altar or meditating in a group. But I don't think running to a class or halting life for an hour to sit is a practical cue-*routine*-reward reset here.

Hmm . . .

This friend is probably not obsessing like I am. She may talk to me when ready . . . but most likely won't. We are emotionally different animals, and that's okay—there's no "right way" to process. And so the kindest thing I can do in this situation—for myself and my friend—is to not wallow in my stormy mind but, instead, to simply *choose not to care so much.* To move on.

So fuck her . . . for now!

"Fuck you too!" Carrie says again the next morning while Mitra and I walk Riverside. Evidently, enlightenment comes slow on this one: I'm stuck on the same emotional conundrum and so have started repeating my Wonder Women when she interjects again. My mental obsession with this tiny squabble is pointless. Carrie knows it. I know it. Together, we cheerlead me again into pulling up my ovaries and tackling my to-do list.

This time it works.

I can better choose what I think and feel.

Carrie Fisher's cursing spunk gifted me this revelation.

I guess timing really is everything in some circumstances. I wouldn't have Carrie on the brain were it not for her recent passing, nor would Wonder Woman be such a Challenge theme were it not for the major motion picture about to come out nationwide, revving women up everywhere. The White House turnover made the incomparable Michelle Obama an obvious name on my list. And if I have two soulmates in the world, human FW Lyndsey and furry rascal Mitra are them. Instinct overruled the overanalyst part of me who would have intentionally plotted a list of traits I wanted to fake-until-I-make. But the extent of Carrie's impact has been entirely unexpected. I ponder the rest of my Wonder Women's unique personal powers:

WONDER WOMAN: a fierce idealist and warrior for peace

CARRIE FISHER: toughen up, lighten up, laugh it off

MICHELLE OBAMA: grace under everything ("When they go low . . .")

FW LYNDSEY ELLIS: bottomless wells of inner strength and character

MITRA: unconditional love is messy, but the greatest force on earth

In the coming week, my mind often stops on the name I need most in a moment. Physical agony keeps me awake one night: Lyndsey helps me trust the moment will pass. Carrie drops the f-bomb so often during self-doubt that I discern I maybe (undoubtedly) care (way) too much about what others (probably don't) think about me. This new coping mechanism helps me compartmentalize and prioritize: I identify emotional triggers, deal with the present, and return when better equipped to think, speak, or act.

But Sunday, January 8, I lie in darkness, unable to sleep.

The Women's March on Washington is January 21.

I *can't go.*

At some point when first sick, my little kid mind started to ponder just how much of life circumstance happens by chance; how a spark of divinity or random conglomeration of cells comes together in a specific time, place, and woman's body. How the era we are born into, the shape and color of skin that encases us, the family that nurtures or abandons us, the opportunities we grow up with or without . . . everything we are results from *that first moment.* I lived in a beautiful house my carpenter father built specifically for us with his own two hands (and team of burly men and machines). I had two parents, three siblings, my own room, and two dogs. A bug bit me, I felt ill all the time, people looked at me differently, and I had no idea what the future held. But my little mind was blown: I was sick, but I was safe.

My father calls me "sensitive." I know I am. But I don't see sensitivity as a weakness. Sensitivity opens us to human kindness and to human suffering; to compassion and action. I often fail in these. I have casually dismissed others. I have let opportunities to take a stand go by. I don't excuse myself. But in a personal goal to "be better tomorrow than I am today," I hope to make small ripples of action that contribute to waves of change.

I'm afraid to fail in this moment.

I'd signed up for the Women's March on Washington in November. But then details began to emerge of the hundreds of thousands expected, the rush of the commute, the route length, the hours of standing . . . With too many physical variables to navigate in the best of circumstances—food, medicine, stimulants, a place to rest—I accept the reality that I am too sick to march.

I am *too sick* to march in support of the health care I've fought so hard to get, retain, and pay for; care I didn't have for years because I have a preexisting condition triggered when I was twelve. *Too sick* to march so that all born with a uterus have access to health care of their choosing. *Too sick* to march for dismantling systemic racism, because skin color does not justify an assumption of anything. *Too sick* to march for tearing down walls that separate humans physically, economically, and socially.

I collapse on my side in the dark bedroom, crying, burning.

I *rail against the disability of my body.*

My inability to act!

I feel disillusioned. I feel abandoned. I feel incensed!

I am suffering. I am spiraling.

I *stop.*

I observe my body, curled in a fetal position, small, powerless.

I take a deep breath, unfurl.

I turn on to my back and open my arms to the sides.

I broaden my hips and spread my legs.

I say, out loud, the names of my Wonder Women.

I breathe and open and repeat.

Eventually, I calm.

Eventually, I focus.

And I think: if I feel this forlorn, chances are others do too.

I don't want to fail through inaction right now.

Dr. Emilie M. Townes is a Baptist clergywoman and the editor of A *Troubling in My Soul: Womanist Perspectives on Evil and Suffering.* A collection of essays by prominent African American womanist scholars and theologians, the group attends to "the shortcoming of traditional feminist and Black theological modes of discourse. The former has a long legacy of ignoring race and class issues. The latter has disregarded gender and class," Townes details.[65] Published in the early 1990s, "shadowed in the inferno and anger of the Rodney King verdict," their discussions are particularly relevant today. They trace how religion, society, and politics discard the suffering of the oppressed. An unarticulated experience that cycles and gets lived over and over, suffering is a sin if "we do not choose to act through our finite freedom on behalf of our liberation from sin to justice," Townes says. "We must learn to move from the reactive position of suffering to that of the transforming power of pain, to use it as a critical stance and refuse to accept the 'facts' handed to us."

I refuse to accept an inability to act.

And nobody owes me anything.

The next morning, I send an e-mail to Allie Cashel and Erica Lupinacci of Suffering the Silence. Suffering the Silence illuminates the life experience of those with chronic illness and disability through art, media, and storytelling. I need their help. I have an idea: what if people going to marches were to carry banners with the photos and names of those in our illness and disability communities? We can match volunteer "Marchers" with "Supporters" unable to attend? We'll design printable banners, and encourage all to connect on social media to increase the visual presence of our community's advocacy?

Allie and Erica respond immediately.

We jump into action.

In a flurry, I write copy for websites and blog posts. Allie designs photo banner templates and sign-up forms. Erica alerts online communities through social media and press. We have so little time. But gratitude replaces powerlessness just at the thought of friends

#MarchingWithMe—the name of our campaign. If only ten others feel that, too, I'll be satisfied with our ripples.

Wednesday, January 11, #MarchingWithMe goes live.

By Thursday, forty volunteers have signed.

I'm waiting on the subway platform, en route to lunch with a colleague, when it all hits: I've helped launch an advocacy campaign and taken an active part in organizing it, plus I'm expending major energy output fielding podcast interviews and writing articles. *Why do I think I'm qualified for this?* I feel a rush of fear. I'm unequipped! I'm one inconsequential human! I'm entirely overwhelmed! I'm . . . berating myself in monologue, without an internal mirror or kind voice to slow me down in response. I subtly shift my stance on the subway platform into a Wonder Woman power pose and gently—*stop*—the thoughts. I cycle my Women and channel Michelle Obama, because I am gonna miss her as First Lady and—*damn!*—can she stay cool through anything. I stay cool through lunch.

An online article about groups compensating for inaccessibility at the Women's March includes #MarchingWithMe. Our list grows. I pose and channel and stay cool during that too.

I drive down to Virginia to spend a few weeks with my First Spouses but return home after only two days because I've caught a cold and can't risk passing it to Lyndsey. I̶ ̶s̶t̶a̶y̶ ̶c̶o̶o̶l̶. No, I don't stay cool about that. I'm heartbroken. But I pose and channel and don't collapse entirely under body-self-loathing.

January 19, I sit at the computer matching Marchers and Supporters. My throat burns, my body aches, my head pounds. I am making myself sicker than I need to be in this moment, I know, punishing myself for being in New York and not Virginia. But photo banners need to be sent by morning so that Marchers have time to print them before traveling to DC or sister marches throughout the country. I organize and match and write two hundred e-mails in six hours. Then I collapse.

January 20, Roomie Erika heads to Washington. In the silence of her absence, I stand, breathe, repeat, and harness gratitude for what we're collectively accomplishing. #MarchingWithMe is not perfect, and we learn as we go. But by evening, social media streams start to fill with partnerships far more loving than I could have anticipated. Supporters share stories about their experiences with illness and disability discrimination; Marchers return with photos of advocacy and action. I feel allied to this monumental moment.

(But still disappointed in my inability to physically march.)

Analytics take a best guess that 4.16 million protestors participate in the Women's March nationwide.[66] I spend the day glued to social media, alternatively reposting for #MarchingWithMe and forcing myself to leave the phone and walk or rest. Leia posters and Wonder Woman costumes fill marches everywhere. Photographer Friend Brent and his wife, Kari, send photos with Lyndsey's and my banners on their backs: I shed tears of flushed gratitude when I see our faces by the National Monument. My Dearie Darling Friend Erin shares another banner with Mitra and me blazing through her (route-approved, clear) backpack and the message: "You and Mitra are fighting the good fight with all of us, my dear." Erin has always come to my side when I'm too sick to venture, and now she carries me with her. My volunteer Marcher, Tracy, posts a photo from San Francisco's pink-tinged City Hall: she carries my banner alongside a poster of Princess Leia with the words: "A Woman's Place Is in the Resistance: We Are Our Only Hope."

My cup overflows with hope.

But alone in my room again, I watch everyone out on the streets together and feel terribly lonely.

This Challenge—this Year—this life—is a process.

It is not perfect.

Neither am I.

#MarchingWithMe ends with around 350 advocates participating nationwide. One participant critiqued that this wasn't nearly enough; in a sea of Marchers, more banners should have flown. Yes. But Michelle Obama didn't become First Lady on a whim and a prayer. Diana didn't become Wonder Woman only when a sword slipped from a stone. Leia could only bring hope to the Resistance after others had sacrificed themselves in battle to bring it to her. Only three years before I first got sick, disability rights advocates abandoned wheelchairs and pulled themselves up the eighty-three White House steps, stunning politicians into finally signing an Americans with Disabilities Act twenty years in the making.[67] Their stones rippled so that I had legal rights to stay in school. Now, #MarchingWithMe only quickly came together because of Allie and Erica's ongoing advocacy with Suffering the Silence. They gave Supporter Sara Barton "an option to feel included and empowered."[68] And Supporter Angela Davis a place at the table so that "working together, we rallied for all of us."[69] Our artists created empowerment images. Our writers penned posts. #MarchingWithMe marches on to other events. Ripples contribute to waves.

Wonder Woman, Carrie Fisher, Michelle Obama, Lyndsey Ellis, Mitra.

They were a stone thrown on January 1.

I finally feel my *it* rippling back.

OVERPOWERED

"Suffering and any discussion that accepts suffering as good are susceptible to being shaped into a tool of oppression. Pain allows the victim to examine her or his situation and make a plan for a healthy future. A position of pain encourages an examination of the past and recovery of the truth. Pain promotes self-knowledge, which is a tool for liberation and wholeness."[70]

I first hear part of this quote from Reverend Dr. Emilie Townes while listening to an online sermon of Reverend Dr. Kathryn Dwyer, the minister at my first spouses' Rock Spring Congregational United Church of Christ. I often listen to Lyndsey's suggestions when restoring in bed or needing a spiritual boost. Filled with curated study, the inclusive, curious, justice-seeking, faith-filled lectures help to sort and make sense of my feelings.

We don't like to talk about suffering, Kathy presents in a sermon on the theme.[71] While pain and suffering are universal, we assume none around us could understand our unique woe. She describes again how religion and politics use suffering as a means to oppress: people suffer either because they have sinned in the eyes of God or are special in the eyes of God; people suffer because it builds character; people suffer in punishment for inherited disobedience. "The effect is like having a neon piece of duct tape placed over your mouth," she says, referring to Chicago-area activists Alex King and D'Angelo McDade. One year after #MarchingWithMe first participates in the Women's March on Washington, the two high school students will step onto the same stage at the March for Our Lives with duct tape covering their mouths. King removes his; he finally has a platform to speak. "Good afternoon, family," he begins. "I say family because of all the pain I see in the crowd. And that pain is another reason why we are here. Our pain makes us family. Us hurting together brings us closer together, to fight for something better."[72]

Pain is not desirable. Suffering is not a virtue.

We rise up when oppressed by it for far too long.

I feel hopeful in our collective action to move beyond it.

But the Monday after the Women's March, I am physically suffering.

Pain overwhelms my body. I wake to learn of a death in the family. #MarchingWithMe and the cold have set productivity back; I owe an editor something that should have been published by now. I *need* to work today. But even mental focus feels like too much. My body begs me to stay in bed and do nothing until restored; until it has energy to tackle family, work, and tending. Instead, I drag to the kitchen and set coffee to perk. I feebly stand in Wonder Woman. Then I sit and tackle one very low hurdle at a time. Later, I Wonder Woman seated at my desk. Debbie Reynolds in my head encourages: "You have to keep striving."

Striving can have us feel alternatively empowered and overpowered.

But yes, Debbie: we have to keep striving.

Around the time I'm implementing this Challenge, Amy Cuddy's power posing TED Talk has forty-two million views. Her book, *Presence*, has topped all the best-seller lists authors want to top. She has a rigorous speaking schedule. And she's been rejected by colleagues in her field of social psychology to such a point that she abandoned her tenure-track teaching position at Harvard.[73]

Cuddy's 2010 study showed that when test subjects posed for one minute each in two high-power poses, they self-reported more confidence. Saliva swabs then revealed a rise in their levels of testosterone, the hormone justifying risk-taking behavior in following test situations. Conversely, those who embodied contracting, low-power poses showed an increase in cortisol (the lovely stress hormone) and were risk-averse.[74] Cuddy's TED Talk, book, and speaking career all flew from these findings: an initial study of only forty-two participants.

Shortly before Cuddy described results in her 2012 TED Talk, psychologists Joseph P. Simmons, Lief D. Nelson, and Uri Simonsohn published a paper exposing rampant false-positive results in studies of social psychology (including their own). When compiling data for reports, researchers make many decisions about sample pools, test environment conditions, methodology, and points of comparative analysis. The trio analyzed data and concluded that researchers far too often prove their hypothesis in the affirmative because "despite the nominal endorsement of a maximum false positive rate of 5 percent (i.e., $p \leq .05$), current standards for disclosing details of data collection and analyses make false positives vastly more likely. In fact, it is unacceptably easy to publish 'statistically significant' evidence consistent with any hypothesis."[75] They called this *p-hacking* (*p* being probability) and singled out studies with p-values higher than 5 percent. Researchers everywhere started to redo studies of their peers, reducing p-values and publishing contrasting results.

Eleven such subsequent studies on power-posing did not garner Cuddy's results. One, led by economics psychologist Eva Ranehill at the University of Zurich with two hundred subjects, did show "a significant effect of power posing on *self-reported* feelings of power," but no hormonal shifts or increased risk-taking behavior.[76]

P-hacking is not new news. Publication bias and priming— where the environment of the study influences a subject's response to stimulus—have been heavily reported since the 1960s. As I read up on neurology and social psychology, I warily notice the concluding phrase "as hypothesized" with alarming regularity. Then, every researcher I get on the phone starts our conversation with a disclaimer; they *know* how much gray lives between the lines of a report. So I look to these studies as I do tarot cards: Tarot Sasha taught me to mix traditional meaning and imagery with my human experience and intuition so to better consider my current scenario from a different perspective.

Can sum curiosities help me reexamine my habits, choices, or direction?

Isn't that what the field of psychology helps us do?

Cuddy's TED Talk had me examine my physicality and question how often I hold my body close in protection. *Could feeling physically small contribute to my feeling emotionally powerless?* After only a few weeks of Wonder Woman, I now self-report an increase in confidence.

But I think back to how Lonely-Hour Julia's loneliness doesn't affect her ability to make big decisions: "It doesn't take a lot to galvanize me into action, frankly," she'd said. "I just sort of up and do some shit." She included launching her podcast as a leap, as well as leaving New York for a new editorial job in Atlanta. I started *Love Bites* on such a creative whim but have stalled a move to a more rural life for years in not knowing where I truly want to be, *happy?*-enough where I am After power posing and repeating my Wonder Women, could an increase in confidence have inspired the launch of #MarchingWithMe? Was it a risk-taking behavior much outside my norm? If power poses don't hormonally increase confidence, what is happening in my body?

I take this to the Wonder Woman who started it all: Marcia Polas.

Marcia is an occupational Pilates teacher for actors, dancers, chefs, and others who use their body in their career. She believes "it shouldn't hurt to do your job": a beautiful testament to how a little time and intention help us live our best lives.

I ask Marcia how an open, welcoming body can increase confidence. Like Designer-Amber, she uses automobiles as an example. When a tire is out of alignment or an engine is sluggish, we work physically and mentally harder on the task of steering the car safely straight down the road. "It's the same idea with your body," she says. When our bodies are misaligned, it's harder to breathe, move freely, or digest. "Whether we realize it or not, we've got energy—and I mean actual calories burned, used, *energy*—going in directions that are not helpful or useful to us," she says. No matter how hard we work, we're never going to achieve as much in a body that's not properly aligned or fully fueled. If we feel uncomfortable in our body, we get distracted and our confidence drops. Those around us on first dates or morning meetings notice. Conversely, when our skeleton is stacked up properly and fully cushioned by muscle, tissue, and fascia, we move it and all systems nestled inside it with ease.

We agree that my specific power poses are most likely insignificant. What matters is the time taken for intention. The expansive position allows my lungs to take in easeful full breath. I notice my body in space. My thoughts naturally go where needed: to my powerful Women or to a mantra made up in the moment. I finish with increased confidence because I've regained control of my thoughts and taken ownership of my body.

What would Marcia suggest for a similarly transformative process?

"Stand with your feet only fist-width apart," she starts. Not wider-than-hip-width—I was wrong in my Wonder Woman stance there—but only fist-width, and balanced equally on both feet. "Squeeze the back of your inner thighs, as if you're pressing on the gas, zero to five—not zero to sixty. You'll feel your butt engage, and your low belly get a little bit stronger. If you can, put your fingertips on the bottom of your sternum. Adjust so that the bottom of your sternum is flat versus kind of sticking up and out; you'll feel your abdominals engage. Then put your hand against your belly button. With your mouth open, inhale very quietly for four counts while pressing your stomach out a little bit into your hand. In your head, say the word *pause*. Then exhale to a count of ten, allowing your stomach to stay exactly where it is in your hand."

I try this, standing while tea water boils.

Past Marcia education has taught me that I (like many of us) hyperextend my chest in a superhero way. As I flatten my sternum—the hard, flat bone in the middle of my chest—I feel an immediate softening in my back muscles. My heart doesn't race; instead, my breath naturally calms. In the release, I feel the power of a neutral center. I feel my muscles engage slightly, which relieves pressure from my joints. As I breathe and count, air stuck in my lungs progressively releases, which Marcia says is a result of our almost constant state of hyperventilation. Plugging into deeper breath, I feel my heart rate slow, my central nervous system calming along with my thoughts. I can't count and cycle my Wonder Women simultaneously, but her pattern blocks out spiraling stress. Counting and pausing, there is only breath and body.

When through, I don't feel ready for battle.

But I feel far fiercer in mind.

Marcia suggests that if we do such regular check-in with our alignment, we then move with greater ease. We invite more oxygen into lungs and cells. We face less distraction. "Then, what else goes easier?" she posits. "What else does my brain have room for?"

A few days before this Challenge's end, I sit at my desk, facing work but battling self-doubt and ennui. The death of my family member—my aunt—has hit Nana particularly hard. I spent the weekend with my grandparents, the three of us not physically able to make the trip south to Georgia for the services. I feel shame at being the sibling once again not there to support my extended family. And sorrow over a genuine want to be. I worry about loved ones in pain, work projects unsold, bank accounts tenuous, and relationships strained.

I don't want to Challenge myself today.

I take Mitra for a walk. I make some tea. I set a two-minute timer, and stand in a softened Wonder Woman. I breathe. I witness the physical sensations in my body. I observe feeling emotionally overpowered by the world. I collect thoughts of how I can best help to empower it instead. I conclude, once again, that the only way to continue on my path is to keep moving forward.

The timer rings.

I take a breath.

And take a step.

A CONFESSION!

I failed at part of this Challenge.

Flat out *failed*.

It's important to me that I fess up about it.

Back when crafting, someone following my journey suggested that "negative thought" wasn't a tangible habit. Easily impressionable, I cobbled logic and decided to also reduce my TV consumption during this time—I spend a lot of time in bed, sick, bingeing, and figured it was an obvious habit I could examine. As I'd be doubling up on Challenges, I figured I could make an attempt at moderation: could I allow myself only one hour of television or one movie per evening?

I originally called this Challenge TELE-WONDER-WOMAN! and led off the month power posing in the morning and hopping into bed at night knowing limited TV time lay ahead. As I couldn't just put on *Gilmore Girls* and fade, every night required a pause for thought: which one movie or episode would I watch for the night? Documentaries hoarded on my queue came to life. Riverside Writers Friend Paul suggested a few series, and sampling each became a game I looked forward to during the day. With hours emptied, I spent more time reading in my corner chair. Books overtook some evenings entirely, and the flat-screen stayed dark and cool. One luscious Sunday, I curled in the corner from dawn to beyond dusk.

But then the month moved on.

I got angry. I got tired. I got sick.

I bent the rules.

I tallied hours banked from TV-free nights and binged a little.

The day after the Women's March, exhausted, I gave in entirely.

I could have admitted a day's defeat and kept going.

But I wanted my television back.

I gave up.

I failed.

Anthropologist-Amber points out that binge-watching used to be an event: we'd rent several videos, buy marathon-intended snacks, and designate breaks for the bathroom and discussion. Now, she says, "You just have a movie marathon every night with Netflix . . . but it's not healthy." I agree . . . to an extent. It's not healthy to stare at a screen when you can read a book, talk to a friend, go for a walk, or interact with the world. But when I can't physically do those things, lying down and being distracted by a world that lifts me out of my pain-ridden body and shows me some happiness is the healthy choice. Even if it's a world I've seen a hundred times before.

Professor David details in an article that one of the reasons we often fail at harnessing self-discipline is because we need optimal environments in which to stay strong. "People whose willpower is taxed fail to resist about one out of every six temptations they face," he relays of one report.[77] If we have too many decisions to make, if we're tired, or if we simply don't have a good enough reason, we give in. I don't watch television out of self-indulgence, laziness, or gluttony. It doesn't distract from the important things I need to do. And so I failed at this Challenge because I didn't *want* to change this habit. I failed because I was eventually too tired to exert willpower against a superficial purpose.

Wait. ~~"I don't watch television out of self-indulgence."~~

I do. But at the end of this failed Challenge, I conclude: there are worse things than a *Supergirl* binge after a day of being a Wonder Woman.

UNCERTAINTY

PHYSICAL BODY: Broadening and opening my body didn't magically create superhero strength. But it did invite more space, thought, and that previously indefinable *it*—my confidence—to return.

SOCIAL INTERACTIONS: No great hippie peace-and-love force flowed through me during social interactions this month. But posing before lunches and phone meetings saved me from showing up disheveled-as-usual. I didn't return home to collapse and cry either. Then there's the new social network still building through #MarchingWithMe. I often stay in the shadows of the chronic illness community, feeling strongly that my illness is only a part of who I am. But there is something to be said for shared experience and optimistic activism. Going *without* this Year, I increasingly contribute to my communities.

SENSE OF SELF: As a result of these, I start feeling a bit more of that elusive "right." I'm not intentionally seeking it anymore. But my sum parts feel a bit more comfortable as we all move together.

***

I take out my tarot deck.

I shuffle three times, cut, and flip the Nine of Swords.

In it, a woman with long black hair sits up in bed, tormented by nightmares. Despite the lush purple and red velvet surroundings, she cannot sleep. Nine swords hover above her. With her eyes closed and swords suspended, she is tortured not by physical force but by the scene that plays out in her mind. It's a beautiful but chilling card. One of anxiety and despair.

One that reminds us that sometimes our torture is of our own making.

Like Townes's conclusions on inactive suffering, the Nine of Swords represents how the more we dwell in nightmares, the more we're responsible for their place in our waking life. We can either let fear and anxiety rule, or we can make a conscious choice to look at our situation objectively (like a card in our hand, perhaps), draw upon our inner strength, and take action. We must lift our face to the darkest hour before we can see the dawn.

I don't believe thoughts magically manifest things into our lives. But I do believe they influence how we communicate with others and make choices. Those then shape our reality.

I don't want to shape from a place of fear, panic, or desperation.

I'd rather fill my body with powerful poses.

And my thoughts with Wonder Women.

At the end of this Challenge, I see the Nine of Swords as

encouragement. My nightly grains of panicked thoughts still swirl, and I don't feel fully free of my sword-tortured nightmares just yet. But now . . .

My eyes are open.

I stare at the swords.

I take action against them.

I keep throwing them down.

Wonder Woman, Carrie Fisher, Michelle Obama, Lyndsey Ellis, Mitra.

And I sleep.

CHAPTER
CHALLENGE **6**

MULTIPLE CHALLENGE!

CHALLENGE: Multiple Challenge!

TIME LINE: Four days

RULES: All past Challenges at once!

In the past, I've started Challenges on Mondays and used any spare days between to plan and regroup. Feeling fiercer of mind, I am no longer cool with that. With four days between major Challenges, I decide to test this sum experiencing-my-experience thing and try all past Challenges at once: no social media, shopping, sugar, (exchanging holiday gifts doesn't really apply), or negative thought. Their totality will require constant self-vigilance.

I'm ready.

Midday Thursday, a hardcore craving for something sweet pings. I've been eating very little sugar since that Challenge ended but haven't recognized such a specific longing in a while. The designated "cannot" inserts an extra pause of thought in the desirous moment. I satiate with hot spiced tea.

In this new period of social media abstention, I find moments of both frustration and profound freedom. The recent apocalyptic drudge of politics has found me lost once again to this very uncalm technology; with #MarchingWithMe's reliance on digital advocacy, I'd almost fallen back into mindless scrolling habits. As Multiple Challenge days pass, the break from online life feels increasingly exhilarating.

Why can't I do this without imposing an official Challenge upon myself?

Why is moderation so much harder than total on or off?

Day Two, I'm not done at my desk until 8:30 p.m. The light outside my window creams together a misty gray-brown like earthenware. The tree branches and iron porch railings that flank the house next door look intensely defined by this light, their pocketed shadows deeply ominous. Across the street, I see some apartment windows glowing orange. Others, pitch black. It's all very *Rear Window*, the kind of evening I love to sit and type inside. The kind I observe because I'm awake and aware, *without* days inviting time for woolgathering without worry.

By Sunday, I come to a decision that feels like a major point of growth: it's time to buy a new laundry bag. From the No Shopping lessons, I've come to better appreciate our time together. But hauling laundry down two flights of stairs, I notice a window-like view of my dirty clothes through the bag's shreds and laugh. That Challenge ended in October. It's now February. It's time.

While my clothes wash, I browse online. I find a durable canvas bag with a bamboo frame for twenty-five dollars. In two days, I'll have one less physical item in my space requiring overexerted energy.

I update Happy-Home Rebecca. "I think it's beautiful that you had to wait for it, because it develops an awareness and an appreciation for the fact that some obstacles are not worth letting be obstacles.

You'll become much more aware of things like that in the future," she says. "I spent a year of my life hating the lock on my front door because it wouldn't open. It's been two years since I fixed it, and I still love opening my door. The contrast—because I had to struggle and struggle—is so poignant, and I think there's really something to take from that."

At the start of My Year, Without, I envisioned that Challenges would be separate and finite. I had no idea I'd *want* any to continue beyond their end dates. I hadn't expected overarching lessons or struggles less superficial than a busted laundry bag or altered bank account. But Rebecca is right: the struggle is poignant. Together, these separate Challenges of *without* create struggle, observation, and appreciation of the entire human that is me.

And tomorrow it all starts over again.

CHAPTER **7**
CHALLENGE

NO WASTE

CHALLENGE: No Waste

TIME LINE: ~~Thirty days~~ Sixty days

RULES: I will not buy anything in packaging that cannot be fully recycled. I will make what I cannot buy, I will not get food delivered. I will only buy secondhand clothes. I will mark how much waste goes out of my home.

ADDENDUM: Medications, supplements, and Mitra's poop bags are allowed.

REFUSE

What do you value?

What does the word *value* even mean to you?

What about *relationships*?

What do your relationships look like?

These are some questions Andrea Sanders asks an audience when introducing the concept of "zero waste." As founder and executive director of Be Zero, Andrea teaches individuals, schools, and communities how to reduce consumer habits that researchers agree tear through our natural resources and flood our landscape with trash.[78] But she doesn't peddle a line of flashy sustainable goods or push to-do lists. Rather, she encourages emotional exploration around our relationship with *stuff*. "No one ever asks the questions, which is probably why most people don't think about it," she explains to me. "What kind of relationships do you have with yourself, with the environment, and with the things you use?" She's found that if we better understand the links between, then we naturally invest in long-term, lower-waste lifestyles.

I started pondering the concept of zero waste a few months ago, when Dear Friend Rebecca suggested I put it on the Challenge list. I'm already an avid recycler. I carry reusable bags and cups. The No Shopping Challenge deepened my relationship with stuff. Before that, so had Happy-Home Rebecca's workshop.

What could a No Waste Challenge look like?

What does zero waste even mean?

According to the Zero Waste International Alliance, "Zero Waste is a goal that is ethical, economical, efficient, and visionary, to guide people in changing their lifestyles and practices to emulate sustainable natural cycles, where all discarded materials are designed to become resources for others to use."[79] The full definition then helps cities, business, and communities set long-term goals in waste reduction.

Then there's the "zero waste lifestyle movement," made visible predominantly (but not only) by white, female bloggers. This force encourages homemade and naturally derived cleaning and beauty products, eschewing plastic, repurposing everything, and purchasing only sustainable products bought in bulk. Many offer goals unachievable for those without excess time, money, physical ability, or access to such goods. Thus, the movement can be viewed as cultural elitism. Others offer easily implemented impactful tips that help all humans significantly reduce waste. There, the guidance is environmental activism. (Within every community, I find both inspiring people and those needing metaphorical light bulbs lit. I try to ask questions until I figure out which an individual is.)

"We all benefit from clean air, water, and resources," Andrea points out. "While we don't live in a perfect system and a lot of things are unjust and not equal, collective attention eases us from thinking, *Well, I can't do everything. What does it matter?*" She doesn't expect everyone to try a zero waste lifestyle. Rather, she hopes we explore our part in the story of "what we collectively value."

What do I value?

I value well-made items. When I see sidewalks going down and buildings going up, I think of the men in my family who lay concrete and stone with purpose and pride. I think of Avó sewing up holes in my jeans, and Nana and Poppa's worn cast iron Dutch oven.

I value the natural world. I hug trees (literally), talk to birds, hush when I spot falcons flying, and never feel more peace than when drifting on a pond.

I value humans. Life is hard. We do the best with what we've got. I try to #BeBetter so that my choices don't make living harder for another.

What do I have?

I have a desire to learn, to change, and to improve. I have time. I have only a small space to maintain. I have just myself to look after. I have access to options.

For thirty days, I'll first use up packaged products already in my home, weighing nonrecyclable trash as it goes out. Then, I'll replace only with fully recyclable or package-free options. I'll buy in bulk. If such an option is not available, I'll attempt to make it myself or go *without*. I'll not get delivery food. Clothing must be purchased secondhand. I don't have access to compost heaps, so I'll be mindful of what I can do to reduce food scraps.

"A circular, zero waste economy is not going to be in our lifetime," Andrea says to calm the nervous ambitions of those starting on a road to waste reduction. "A lot of the things we're doing may seem small and insignificant, but they create the ripples."

I'm all about ripples.

But as I sit in contemplation, I tap into a fear beyond the surface disposability of stuff: Am I *a disposable person*? Is my lack of a relationship or my inability to secure financially sustaining work a mark of my low value? Is my continued loss of health a sign my body is giving up on me too?

If so, can I increase the value of my humanity?

And can wasting less show me how?

MY STORY OF STUFF

I again find myself a frog-in-a-boiling-pot of modern convenience.

Evidently, while I was in college, angry with the Internet, the popularity of e-mail was starting to dwindle the US Postal Service's letter-carrying business. To compete with shipping companies, USPS shifted government-regulated subsidies to package delivery; as long as bodies continued to sort and deliver whatever was brought to facilities, quotas could be met. Because Amazon has warehouses within easy distance to stations, they save huge in shipping costs, and we get affordable two-day delivery.[80] Other companies pushed to compete. As a result, plastic shrink-wrap, foam peanuts, and air cushions now fill our trash. New York City basements overflow with delivery boxes.[81]

I'm charged to change my part in the collective.

So I lean right into the hippie clichés of this Challenge.

On a sunny Sunday morning, I head to markets with my cloth bags, ready to stock up on things I normally have delivered. I buy bulk coffee and almonds. I hawk-eye prices. My ego thrills at this lifestyle shift, until I wonder if my bird-brain is missing something? Zero-waste bloggers promise that bulk buying saves money. But the least expensive comparable coffee I find is a two-dollar-per-pound hike from my favorite packaged blend; the almonds a *seven-dollar-per-pound upgrade* from the tub I get delivered.[82] Nourishing food is a health cost I already struggle to absorb. I take fair-trade and small businesses into consideration when I buy, too, and know where to find the most affordable blend of these values online and in stores.

How will my wailing wallet recoup from this no-packaging hit?

A bit disenchanted, I find sea sponge tampons to replace my regular (applicator-less) brand, calculating it will take six months until I'm saving money. (Plus, they come in a plastic package.) After schlepping to four stores, I give up on finding cloth handkerchiefs to replace tissues. At home, I find brushed cotton hankies sold by the same woman on both Etsy and Amazon. Etsy delivery takes two weeks; Amazon, two days. I live for today. I feel guilty for tomorrow.

What do I value?!

The Challenge begins.

The following Sunday, I'm shocked to weigh only five ounces of nonrecyclable trash: produce bags, a foundation pump, a potato chip bag, a plastic tape dispenser, nonrecyclable caps, plastic meat wrap, and a plastic baby toothbrush Mom gave me to try on Mitra (fail!). I assess that I prepped a lot of food for my first week and so didn't really use up all that much. But the second Sunday, I'm down to three ounces. I haven't gone shopping again and realize I might last the entire thirty days this way. I decide to extend a second month.

As the weeks pass, I fill plastic quart containers (repurposed from past delivery soup) with olive oil, freshly churned almond butter, more coffee, and loose vegetables. No matter how many markets I hit or how many coupons I source, my wallet takes the hit. This happens week after week.

I try to focus on gratitude for food.

Then things start to shift.

One day, I finally make it to a Harlem butcher shop I've long wanted to try. I stock up on gorgeous grass-fed meat, eggs, and butter. The bill is shockingly *less* than what I would have spent via my old routine. Plus, I bring it home wrapped only in paper, completely free of Styrofoam or plastic. I cook with glee.

I run out of toothpaste. I execute a blogger's simple recipe and will never need a thick plastic tube again!

I run out of a few spices. I recognize my food writer's unused excess, clear out, and replace only vital items!

I run out of foundation and try a natural brand in low-waste packaging. My skin feels great!

I *don't* run out of lipstick because I have not-perfect colors still lingering after the No Shopping tackle. I clear those out too. They look smashing on the ladies who come over to watch the Super Bowl. (Roomie Erika's doing; I don't know a 5K from a ten-yard pass.)

I make almond milk. The process is messy and costs 70 percent more per cup than my preferred brand, delivered with a nonrecyclable cap. But it tastes creamy and sweet, and with time, I learn to enjoy the meditative fifteen minutes during which I blend, strain, and press almonds and water into milk.

Which things do I value more than others?

In Connecticut, with two weeks to the finish line, I sit once again dreamy and distracted, gazing out the picture window in front of my desk. Tree branches stand bare against the blue sky. Eighteen inches of snow cover the yard. Sun and wind together have smoothed every trace of rough stone wall or hill into one gently rolling plain. My hammock fights its frozen chains to slightly swing. Mitra sleeps on a bed at my side, my hand brushing over her warm body comforting us both. I hear only our breath within and the wind without. Trees start to sway; first my favorite white oaks in the yard, then those deeper in the woods. "You know I've always been a tree worshipper," my literary kindred spirit Anne Shirley whispers in my mind. I smile. In my renewed dedication, I feel more connected to this earth than ever before.

But . . . *It's not enough.*

While this Challenge has largely cut down my use of nonrecyclable materials, my recycling haul has increased. Single-use plastic, paper, and items that come in cardboard—made from the beautiful trunks of the trees I profess to worship—have still brought *stuff* into my space. I've not considered raw materials in prioritizing *recycle* over *reduce*!

This is exactly what "they" want us to do.

A 1955 report by economist Victor Lebow is often referenced when illuminating how consumerism became the US economic plan post World War II. "Our enormously productive economy demands that we make consumption our way of life, that we convert the buying and use of goods into rituals, that we seek our spiritual satisfactions, our ego satisfactions, in consumption," Lebow says.[83] Recognizing a need for a new economy in postindustrial America, government programs started to purport an American Dream of extrinsic goals. "We need things consumed, burned up, worn out, replaced, and discarded at an ever-increasing pace," Lebow explained. To establish such a hedonic treadmill, advertisements and sales would need to push spending rituals with a sense of urgency; more of Selfridge's "[so many] days until Christmas."

How do politicians measure our country's stability today?

Not by our subjective happiness, no.

But by whether or not we're spending.

By the 1970s, municipalities had to hire private waste management companies to haul away increased garbage as a result.[84] Instead of reversing the tide against gluttonous consumerism, beverage and packing companies pushed for increased recycling programs. Before the 1980s, recycling rates were negligible. Then, the school specials I remember vividly from childhood trained us to think we were doing good so to expressly allow more single-use items to get made without our realizing the damaging environmental effect.

"The growth of plastics production in the past sixty-five years has substantially outpaced any other manufactured material," a recent worldwide report states. "The same properties that make plastics so versatile in innumerable applications—durability and resistance to degradation—make these materials difficult or impossible for nature to assimilate."[85] In 2014, United States citizens threw away 258 million tons of trash; only 89 million tons (34.6 percent) of the paper, plastic, textiles, or food scraps within were recycled or composted.[86] Most of us don't know exactly what, where, or how we can recycle. Or we don't even bother trying.

I worry I may have transported misguided habits across state lines.

I start digging for details.

Recycling is mandatory in both Connecticut and New York; businesses and individuals are required by law to separate out recyclable goods, and if a company offers trash collection, they must also collect recyclables.[87] In New York, we separate paper from plastic, metal, and glass. Our Connecticut provider offers "single stream" recycling, where all can go in together. At single stream plants, humans separate cardboard and glass, then massive machines use magnets to extract tin and steel, spinners to toss out paper, and eddy current to eject aluminum. These then separately get bulked and sold as commodity items (things with market value). In best-case scenarios, companies then buy the bulk and turn them into raw materials that get repurposed. The higher quality material, the better chance the lot has of selling. In worst-case scenarios, the materials don't get sold and go to the dump.

Our action plays a part. Tossing in nonrecyclable goods increases sorting costs, therefore decreasing the benefit to the provider. Grease-covered pizza boxes and peanut butter–crusted jars aren't hot commodities; washing our goods helps. Then, the more we buy things made from recycled materials, the greater value the materials have.

With so many kinds of plastics out there and various recycling technologies, I find conflicting city guides. It ends up, I'm wrong in my no-cap assumption: in 2013, many cities started accepting a wider range of plastics, including the lids I was taught to remove and trash. (I don't need to be making almond milk!) But the spread of information is slow, and where I've lived in New York, Connecticut, and Ohio all work differently. Municipalities that focus on educating their communities and offering ready access to recycling show higher "diversion rates"; the percentage of recyclable trash diverted from landfills. A national goal is 35 percent. San Francisco has the highest, at around 90 percent;[88] various studies place New York City around 17 percent. But even best-case scenarios aren't perfect. We can't control the future carbon footprint of raw materials. And all waste management requires resources of gas, oil, water, and electricity.

Isn't it simpler to reduce?

"Simplicity is about always evolving," Be-Zero Andrea says. "Stuff is energy. Having a lot of stuff can overwhelm and distract us."

I think back to what Pilates Marcia said about how a misaligned body wastes energy. And Happy-Home Rebecca's thinking that a busted laundry bag is not the best place for energy either. And Anthropologist-Amber's "panic architecture" energy overwhelm. And my deciding not to waste energy I don't have on unfulfilled conversations or unused stuff.

But what about the energy required of natural resources and the human hands I claim to value? It's not the thought that counts here—it's action. Beyond this Challenge, can I actively craft a habit of reduction? Of refusal? Can I reduce my use of single-use cups and buying two when I only need one? Can I refuse straws and sample-size cosmetics? Can I forgo markers of memories and instead invest in relationships and the memories themselves?

I will try.

Because I, too, am a tree worshipper.

I refuse to no longer act on it.

THE ONLY HABITABLE PLACE

I walk into my kitchen, sick and sore, and pause in the doorway.

Morning light pours in, refracting and reflecting the sun in prisms and rainbows on to counters and over appliances. Standing there, I almost see another version of myself, moving in this same kitchen on an alternate plane of time and space. I watch her. She smiles as she hand-washes handkerchiefs, hanging them in the sunlight to dry.

She blends almonds and water into milk with movements quick and determined. She rinses vegetables and sorts bags of coffee, nuts, and meat procured from an easeful excursion to the farmer's market. I see her—that other me—through this veil of light that barely separates our worlds. In both, our spirits embrace these Challenge activities. But her whole body joyfully executes them. As I step into my very real kitchen, my body rails, a physical Challenge in motion. I wring handkerchiefs and the muscles in my back burn. The scrape of blending almonds threatens the migraine I've tempered for days. I keep the lights low while sorting goods I struggled to bring home.

This real world hurts.

One evening in Connecticut, I almost black out in a store. I drop my intended purchase, race to lie in the car, and let the world spin. The next night, again: I grab some food in plastic and run before I fall.

In New York, I thrill at what I find in that Harlem butcher shop. But my body burns under the weight of bringing it home. I cannot afford a cab. There is no direct bus or subway. I shift the load, struggling from one long block to the next. I land home feverish and overwhelmed.

The cold that started in January won't leave. Dad drives me to a doctor. Bro' Dan drives me home. Antibiotics make my standard symptoms worse. I fall into a bus stop walking Mitra. Mom brings medicine, sorbet, and flowers wrapped in plastic. Bro' holds Mitra hostage until I can walk straight again.

These struggles don't diminish Challenge triumphs.

But is waste another health cost I have to accept?

"The world doesn't owe me anything," FW Lyndsey says when I ask how she manages. "Just because I have an illness doesn't mean I'm entitled to any resource I get my hands on."

Hers is an uncommon sentiment in a time when entitlement floods public conversation. It's an opinion we share, among many

other things. Yes, a history of illness connects us; we both first
fell sick in our preteen years, and a few symptoms and diagnoses
overlap. But more so, our souls collide because of shared joy in
the complexity of daily living. We talk for hours on the phone in
conversations never long enough. We regularly update each other
on the changing wildlife in our urban neighborhoods. When side-
by-side, we stroll into a nearby forest and observe boulders, moss,
light, air, and animals with Anne Shirley–like dreamy identification.
"When we can't go far, we go deep," Lyndsey once poetically
concluded.

"I have often felt like the world—meaning not people necessarily
but our natural world—shouldn't have to pay for the fact that I have
an illness," she tells me now of her perspective on waste. "It shouldn't
have to absorb the negative externality."

I ask her to detail the "negative externality"—the cost suffered by
a third party because of her illness—because of where we differ: in
severity of illness, and in educational and professional background.

Lyndsey and Christian met at Brandeis University while getting
their masters in sustainable international development. Lyndsey
went on to monitor and evaluate programs in the international
development sector; Christian works as a policy adviser in
international development. They bring a swath of knowledge from
these into their lifestyle. Through observation, I've witnessed how
intention and action truly make a difference.

Lyndsey had Hodgkin's lymphoma as a child—a form of cancer
none survived before the aggressive treatment given to those in her
generation. Late effects of that pediatric lymphoma evolved into
primary immunodeficiency disease, blood clots, autoimmune issues,
and endocrine issues. These fill her days with widespread symptoms,
doctors' appointments, and extremely complicated treatments.

Every night, she runs intravenous fluids into her body through a system of bottles, vials, needles, and tubes that need disinfecting and inserting in specific order. She gives herself nightly blood thinner injections. Twice a week, she sets up a different system to inject immunoglobulins; made from the plasma of thousands of donors, they help her immune system recoup what it does not produce on its own. No matter how tired, bruised from needles, or beleaguered by symptoms, she somehow repeats these with grit, strength, humility, and humor. Week after month after year.

The negative externality comes in mounds of posttreatment waste.

Every week or so, a medical company delivers a Styrofoam cooler packed with ice packs and bags of IV fluid. Massive boxes of needles, tubes, glass bottles, wipes, drop cloths, syringes, and batteries come into, get used, and must then leave her space. Never has anyone in the medical field begun a conversation about the waste. "Not only do professionals not lead on this, but they're way behind," she explains. Visiting nurses throw everything away immediately. "They don't think about it."

Lyndsey and Christian do.

No one could blame them for trashing it all at the end. Instead, they separate all used goods. Sharps (needles) go into a medical box they must legally mail to a facility. Hard plastics and paper products, including the backing strips of plastic packaging, go into their building's recycling program. They take soft plastics to MOM's Organic Market—a nearby market with a detailed community recycling program. MOM's also recycles their plastic bags and batteries. They repurpose drop cloths for things that need moisture absorption, like under dripping air conditioners. Then they drive the Styrofoam coolers, plastic shipping air packs, and ice packs to their local UPS store, which promises to reuse them.

The only things they trash are tubing, IV bags, and alcohol swabs.

"It's been a kind of a work in progress," Lyndsey says of figuring out what could go where. A representative from Arlington County Department of Environmental Services confirms for me that their diversion rate was 46.8 percent in 2016; that program significantly helps.[89] But Lyndsey had to call the DES several times to determine recycling specifics, down to the lids of medicine vials or syringes without needles. MOM's fills in the gaps. Run by the ethos "To protect and restore the environment," their recycling program diverted 48,224 pounds of batteries and 2.3 million pounds of cardboard and prevented the daily use of 5,694 plastic bags in 2017.[90] Their website makes clear what they recycle, the recycling companies they send items to, and how those items then get processed. A dedicated web page describes "Core Values" in a Be-Zero Andrea kind of thought process: "Being fortunate is a state of mind." "Esteem comes from doing esteem-able acts." "Growth is a process, not an event." "Be a voice, not an echo."

Throughout our conversation, Lyndsey instinctively tallies both accessibility and challenge: she has a car in a garage, but driving exhausts her. MOM's is now a block away, but before, they drove troves to a distant location. With individual UPS franchises determining reuse programs and no formal confirmation, she can only hope they uphold their end of the bargain; the coolers and ice packs are extremely heavy to transport. "Most people aren't going to be able to physically deal with materials," she recognizes. "I think for some who are very ill, their only option is to throw a big bulk of it away."

She also acknowledges many don't have the mind-set and that she has a passionate partner in Christian, who finds resources when her leads run dry. "I might have a new piece of plastic we can't figure out how to recycle," she describes. "When I'm tired or we get a little bit lazy, we have stopped over the garbage but then been like, 'Oh, *but the sea turtles!*' We both have this image of a sea turtle getting *that* piece of plastic in its mouth. And we're like, '*Nope, we can do this. We'll do whatever it takes to recycle this plastic.*'"

We laugh: I at the idea of her and Christian being "lazy"; I assume she at the sentimentality of this imaginary turtle. (But the truth is no joke; plastic pollution in waterways has harmed 86 percent of sea turtle species and 267 marine species worldwide.[91])

I've witnessed many times how Lyndsey calls in orders, accepts boxes, unpacks goods, organizes systems, utilizes setups, breaks down waste, and recycles each bit of this medical material. I've also known her at the furthest brink of unbearable physical pain.

"It's something I can do," she says.

This Wonder Woman of mine.

She is the stone; I am her ripple.

She is the voice; I am her echo.

But I don't know how to move forward in my body today.

In the introduction to his study "Law for the Ecological Age," Dr. Joseph H. Guth says nothing is more important than placing great value in our Earth because "it is the only habitable place we know in a forbidding universe."[92] Once we destroy this one, we're done. I think of our bodies as the same; they are the only vessels we get for the duration of our living days.

I have a month of this Challenge left. I'm in pain. I still can't drive. (While I'm sick in bed, my car gets towed and Bro' Dan has to yell at me before I'll accept help from him and Dad in retrieving it. I'm still learning how to receive.) I don't have a partner or nondelivery resources to help with bulk options. I don't want to give in or give up.

Lyndsey works with fierce protection to sustain her habitable place. She knows my stubborn tendencies often come at a cost to my body. She gently encourages compromise.

I shift the rules.

I place a grocery delivery order for heavy items almost entirely in recyclable materials. Another sunny Sunday, I collect light bulk items on foot. Instead of beating myself down for another make-believe test my body lost, I put my faith again in long-term change.

"Even though I have an illness, I still owe the natural world to be the best steward I can be," Lyndsey says.

I, too, promise to be the best steward I can be to the habitable places that are my beautiful, ailing body and this beautiful, abused earth.

MELLOW **YELLOW**

Two hundred and forty-four days into shifting habits, I observe a new pattern in my mornings.

I naturally rise early. Fragrant hot coffee sits waiting, readied with intention the night before. I Wonder Woman at the window while almond milk warms, taking in the early morning light. It's brighter than it was a month ago. I notice this because I now notice everything. I pour a cup and sit at a readied desk. Against the glow of a late-winter sunrise, I first whisper the prayer of manifestation printed in front of me, calling in abundance and banishing defeatist thoughts. Then I shuffle, cut, and contemplate one tarot card to guide my day.

Now, I am ready.

I glance at my to-do list, then type, research, and work. Mitra pawing at my leg is the signal it's time to walk. I don't take my phone. Or I take it, but it naturally stays in my pocket. (How far I've come since last summer!) I check in with the sky. Birds chirp slightly more today than yesterday. I say hello to neighbors and hug dogs I know by name. Two sets of front doors separate a vestibule in my building. As I approach them, I see an entrapped pigeon trying to take flight. Oh!—my brain warns!—*it will smash itself into the wall!* But it is only a reflection. I watch the pigeon pull up into the sky behind me, as if I'm peering into a surreal looking glass of bright blue. How miserable to have missed that moment were my face lost in a phone.

I smile.

I am still sick, single, and broke.

But I am happy,

Happy, comma!

I know *happy. period* is out there.

But this comma was a long time coming.

Back in January, I'd participated in Hypnotherapist-Higgins's New Year workshop. Guided meditations and journal prompts helped us recount past goals and plot desires for the coming year. Sinking deep into meditation one day, I asked spirit guides and angels and my subconscious (I'll take whoever I can get) for messages. I tried to envision a life where I feel most present, true, and strong and was shown a familiar "future me"—for I've seen her many times before—in a humble woodland house, gazing calmly out at trees. She has quiet in which to think and work. She has space in which to move. She has time. Her energy doesn't focus on *doing*, just on *being*. Sinking further, I asked my subconscious where I might be resisting the change that would bring this vision into reality. I heard: *Further than ever from a healthy body, stable bank account, or loving romantic partner, you do not consider yourself worthy of this life.* I then approached my future self with tears streaming. She promised I am, indeed, deserving and shouldn't be afraid to take action toward the life I want. A yellow glow then filled my body. The color of the third chakra, I learn it correlates to cultivating confidence and moving from inertia to action.

Yellow was to be my color in the new year.

Confidence the *it* I take back.

So as I've contemplated Wonder Women and the value of stuff, I've also surrounded myself with yellow: I wear golden jewelry, my gold Ganesh and Mother Mary take central spaces on my desk, and my screensavers fill with yellow images. In morning meditation, I ask for love, health, and work with increasing wholeheartedness. I set a goal to borrow a woodland house next winter, to give my body a place to restore during trying northern months. I ask for a loving, strong, sexy, smart-as-hell man to walk with me on this path to somewhere. I ask to be present, if only so to *be* when my body can't *do*.

It took time.

But months later: single, sick, broke, and *happy, comma*.

I've wanted a golden Wonder Woman power suit of sorts, but I don't own any yellow clothing. Mid–March, I contemplate: what part do clothes play in the value of this Challenge? During the No Shopping stint, I learned inherited and thrift finds are my favorites. I'm good at giving to friends or donating unwanted wearable goods, and only throw out those too stained or worn. But where do my practices fit in with the bigger picture?

"People want to feel a connection to the brands they're purchasing from and the products they're using," says Lindsey Rupp, the Bloomberg reporter. She tells me we're a lot less brand-loyal than we used to be; fashion trends haven't much changed, and so "people don't necessarily care where something comes from unless there's a brand that speaks to them in an authentic way." For those in my demographic, transparent sourcing helps consumers invest in clothes of better quality, made in better working conditions, and with less waste. She calls back to our childhood, where having the same brand as everyone else signified coolness: "Now, you build your own aesthetic," she says. "What you wear, buy, and post online says a lot about you and who you are, and you want it to be unique." The rise in cottage-industry fashion sold online and through platforms like Etsy helps us create our unique looks and challenges large, cheap competitors, "allowing sort of death by a thousand cuts" she describes.

I can't buy new clothes for a little while longer. What about thrift?

Because of our buy-and-toss habits, the United States weighs in around twenty-four billion pounds of nondurable textile waste a year. That's seventy-five pounds of clothes, shoes, and draperies *per American*.[93] In a quick online dig, I find while 95 percent of textiles are fully recyclable commodity items, we only recycle 18 percent—I feel like a fool; my assumptions are wrong again! Large thrift organizations *want* the unwearable goods I toss. They resell 10 to 20 percent of donations, then bulk and sell the rest by weight to companies that either ship them overseas or recycle them into things like insulation or furniture padding.[94]

But haven't I decided *reduce* is best?

To connect textiles to everything I've learned about recycling and hedonic slow death, I try to track the life cycle of a cotton T-shirt (since we use and discard so many).

Cotton crops require immense amounts of water to grow, plus pesticides and herbicides that threaten the environment and people I so value. Then, gigantic gas-guzzling machines harvest, separate, bale, and ship the cotton to faraway factories in China or India. There, more massive machines work cotton into yarn, weave yarn into sheets, and color sheets with dyes often containing carcinogenic elements like cadmium and lead, and other byproducts that pollute air and waterways.[95] The sheets then go to factories in nearby countries like Bangladesh, where around four million people cut and stitch T-shirts in monstrous conditions.[96] In 2013, a building containing five garment factories collapsed, killing 1,100 Bangladeshis and injuring 2,500 more.[97] Years later, safety measures preventing such tragedy are still not in place and the minimum wage sits at thirty-two cents an hour.[98] The T-shirts then get shipped and trucked to where we find them. Finally, most of us throw the shirt away in half the time we did a few decades ago.[99]

The thing that frosts my cookies? The shirt's planned obsolescence.

To keep us on that hedonic treadmill, the fashion industry intentionally makes cheap clothes that fall apart fast: "Nondurable goods generally last less than three years," an EPA report concludes.[100] New styles in windows pressure us to keep up; we buy five times more clothing items than we did back in the 1980s,[101] and global clothing production doubled between 2000 and 2014. The fashion industry is now responsible for 10 percent of all global carbon emissions,[102] second only in pollution to the oil industry.[103] I calculate my fifteen dollar T-shirt takes some forty-seven hours for a factory worker to buy.

Forget about if I'm a disposable person.

In our habit of consume-and-discard, have we made all life disposable?

The final misty Saturday before the Challenge ends, I'm waiting for prescriptions in our Connecticut town center and start to ponder the nearby Turnover Shop Mom mentions like a skipping record every time this Challenge comes up. I haven't been inside in years. I remember it as sort of old and disorganized; a clutter of clothes and housewares cramped under fluorescent lighting with the slightly sour musk of the aged. Purchases help raise money for local nursing home care and the Parent Teacher Association. This *is* my community . . .

I cross the street to look . . . just in case.

Inside it is, indeed, cramped and glowing an odd yellow-blue. Clothes pack together, tight and disorganized. I start pushing hangers down the line. My eyes catch color. I crack a smile and collect a small stack. I duck into a dressing room. Ten minutes later, I leave with three yellow sweaters, all in excellent condition, bought for twenty-six dollars.

Was it really that easy?

It starts to rain. With time still to kill, I treat myself to a counter lunch of chicken soup, french fries, and hot black coffee at the diner next door. I keep my phone in my pocket. I look out at the gray.

I think hard on this Challenge's end.

If I truly value human life and my habitable places, then I have to keep improving my story of stuff. If I don't, I might as well feed plastic to Lyndsey's turtles, chop down my favorite white oaks, and stop pretending I am someone I'm not. It's too easy to make significant changes: to swap clothes with friends, to do fewer loads of laundry, to recycle unwearables, to buy secondhand, and to commit to better brands. I know in more ways than six Challenges now that temporary, cheap fixes only Band-Aid, costing everyone dearly in the long run. Lower-waste habits won't always be convenient, but they will get me closer to that calm, present, strong future self I see calling from every meditation.

I can only #BeBetter tomorrow if I act today.

I finish my soup and coffee. The remaining fries fit in a small paper bag I will reuse (and then recycle). It's now cold and raining hard.

But I foresee a bright spring coming, glowing in gold.

And me, a touch more confident.

And content with *happy, comma.*

INDISPOSABLE

PHYSICAL HEALTH: Accepting my body's limitations, I learn to trust ripples and echoes. I focus on sustainable long-term goals. *Evolve* becomes a big word in my self-self-help playbook.

SOCIAL INTERACTIONS: I wonder if I've taken part in what Be-Zero Andrea calls "quiet activism"? In refusing single-use products, bringing reusable dishware everywhere, and Instagramming almond milk and toothpaste updates, might I activate others? "You never know what seeds you're planting," she says.

SENSE OF SELF: The habitable place that is my body has limited energy. The habitable place that is our earth has limited energy. Stuff is energy. I need more energy. I want less stuff. I yearn to apply better practices to even more of my space, but funds and shared city living make this complicated. "You have to tap into a sense of contentment," Happy-Home Rebecca coaches. "I think in our very high-achieving culture, we are always on to the next goal. And that's very unhealthy, right? Find ways to approach your ideal each day." I keep those long-term goals in mind and spend some woolgathering time envisioning how I can bring a little of my future self into my present world.

***

At the top of this Challenge, I wrote in my journal:

"I think this also comes from an emotionally rooted issue of worrying I'm a disposable person; I don't matter to others, so they feel they can easily dispose of me. I don't want to be that. I want to be a person of value. I want to matter so much that people think twice about losing me. Ouch."

Fifty-five days later, I sit on my rug with my ancient vacuum cleaner and a paring knife. The vacuum's foot has dangled pathetically for months, barely usable. I jigger it off. I deftly separate years of dirt and hair from its thin grooves. I needle the long screw back through wires and wheels; it might hold until I find a replacement part. It takes twenty minutes of grossly satisfying work. But when I finish, the foot slides and sucks smoothly. There are smarter vacuums to be bought now, for sure. But why landfill heavy metal and plastic for no reason?

Satisfied, I climb into bed and open a stack of journals from college I've salvaged from the basement. Pressed inside are love letters, scribbled refrigerator magnet poetry, song lyrics, and haikus. Then, I unfold a seventeen-year-old letter from Ben. We were only one year into our blossoming friendship. But from what I can gather of his delicate scrawl, I'd been contemplating school abroad and worried our intimacy would dissipate if I left. Then his promise:

"You are 300 percent wrong about being replaceable . . . There will never be another you."

I had thought my recent fears of disposability a new revelation; a reaction to being sick, single, and broke in my thirties. Evidently, I'm letting a very old wound air and properly heal. I didn't go abroad back then. Instead, I moved from the dorm into a house on a lake, with Lyndsey. Two years later, I got a mint-green stick vacuum.

Fifteen years on . . .

If I can still enjoy cleaning that scrappy old vacuum?

If I can savor simple pleasures?

If I can thrill at yellow sweaters and messy homemade toothpaste?

If I feel calmer and more *happy, comma* with every passing day?

If I have Ben and Lyndsey despite decades of our collective struggles?

If my friendships and my vacuum are not disposable? . . .

Then neither am I.

CHAPTER
CHALLENGE **8**

NO HUSTLE

CHALLENGE: To face head-on the lack of success in my freelance work life, I'll Challenge the habits surrounding it. I'll remove those that most create the scaffolding around my workdays and observe how attention, motivation, and productivity shift in their absence.

TIME LINE: Four weeks (twenty-eight days)

RULES: Week One: No Coffee

Week Two: No Television

Week Three: No Comfy Clothes "To Work"

Week Four: No Working Past 5:00 p.m.

SKINT

I fell hard for *Gilmore Girls*.

I never saw its original airing in the early aughts. Instead, it was love upon now-available-on-Netflix first episode. That November of 2015, I'd work to exhaustion, anticipating a beloved brownie-and-binge reward. When finally ensconced with chocolate and flat screen, no body pain, dating failure, or shoddy paycheck mattered, because Lauren Graham's overly caffeinated Lorelai Gilmore assured me that nothing too bad would happen in the next forty-four minutes. Night after night, I vicariously drank martinis, ate inhuman amounts of Chinese food, expressed big emotions, and always made the hard call. Work angst? Mid-thirty-something dating conundrum? Friend or family squabble? Lorelai was smart. Lorelai was resourceful. She would figure it out. She would work to make it right. In my sick, scared solitude, I *needed* her humor and heart. And so I blew through the entire seven-season series—153 episodes—in a little over three months.

Almost a year later, Netflix announced a four-episode reboot, and I eagerly anticipated matured humor and hope. When it finally launched during my dark No Sugar Challenge days, I instead saw fear, pain, and vulnerability reflecting back my life's frustrations like a mirror, instead of a screen.

Ten years since we'd last seen them, daughter Rory is now closer to my age than mother Lorelai. She'd closed the original series a high-achieving recent Yale journalism graduate following Barack Obama's senate campaign trail. When we pick up, she's a freelance writer naming big publishing bylines, jetting regularly to London, and eating in fancy restaurants with clients and hotshot friends. She looks gorgeous and sounds smart. But we quickly learn that Rory's not landing any new stories. She has no money. When night anxiety keeps her from sleeping, she tap-dances her mind calm. She eventually moves in with her mother. "I'm flailing, and I don't have a plan, or a list, or a clue," she melts down.

If Rory can't make it—with her Ivy League education and pedigreed circle—then what hope is there for me?

I'm bothered as I watch. Because unlike Lorelai's constant drive to fix her Everywoman struggles, Rory lets all burn around her. She falls asleep while interviewing sources. She spends all of two minutes pondering an idea for a major media outlet. She doesn't prepare for a potential editorial job interview. Early in the series reboot, *The Atlantic* drops her (fictional) story. After the series aired, real-life *Atlantic* editor Megan Garber reflected, "Maybe our fictional editors simply discovered that Rory Gilmore, her gleaming résumé notwithstanding . . . is not a very good journalist. That she might even be, actually, an actively bad journalist."[104]

Yes, I'm bothered by the reboot. But is that fair?

Am I really doing any better in reality than Rory is in fiction?

There's something to be said for the freelance writer's life: the schedule flexibility, regular time with Mitra, and lack of dress code. But there's also significant risk: no income regularity, health care, comforting schedule stability. I am my boss and my own assistant. I pitch, apply, research, interview, write, copyedit, upload, rewrite, invoice, publicize, and promote. I field constant rejection. I chase down paychecks. I am to credit for my success and to blame for my failure. I constantly employ systems so to instill work-life structure in my home-life space.

This takes self-discipline.

This takes self-care.

This takes stretch pants.

This takes a *Gilmore Girls* amount of coffee.

But do my systems help or harm my bottom line?

I don't have one master habit I think may best address this significant deliberation. So this month, I'll change up small habits that might shift some scaffolding around my productivity. I'll take them on for one week each: coffee, television, wearing comfy clothes "at work," and working after 5:00 p.m. Simple in theory, all might prove quite the Challenge, given how many hours I spend at my desk.

I wonder how long the Girls would last.

DECAFFEINATED

No Coffee

I could blame my coffee habits on the Gilmores. (They're clearly addicted.)

But I don't even know how much coffee I drink regularly.

Two cups some days? Four others? None on Sundays?

"Caffeine is chemically similar to the neuromodulator adenosine, which accumulates through the day and induces drowsiness for sleep at night," explains an article from the American Psychological Association.[105] Because they're similarly structured, caffeine can bind to adenosine and block our brain from feeling sleepy. At best, caffeine gives us immediate dopamine-releasing side effects of energy and alertness.[106] At worst, if our bodies are particularly sensitive or we've fallen into excess and addiction, it can cause headaches, shakiness, depression, anxiety, sleep disorders, brain fog . . .

According to the Mayo Clinic, there can be anywhere between 95 and 165 milligrams of caffeine in an eight-ounce cup of brewed coffee, depending on how the beans are roasted and brewed.[107] A report on the effects of caffeine compiling data from 380 studies concludes that around four hundred milligrams a day is healthy for nonpregnant humans who don't show obvious sensitivity.[108]

So coffee is awesome for a chick with fatigue issues and a job!

But not for the same babe with brain fog, night anxiety, and migraines?

Do I have a healthy habit or a dangerous addiction?

I started drinking coffee regularly during one rather recent dietary testing stint that forbade tea, my beverage of choice. That's also when I discovered the thrill of the preset function on drip coffee pots found in households everywhere. I suspect my coffee habit is a result of large-pot ease, not addiction. But as this Challenge will allow me to drink tea—which contains only thirty to ninety milligrams of caffeine per cup (depending on tea and brew) comparatively—I'm about to find out.

Monday morning, I pour water over Earl Grey tea leaves and swirl in homemade almond milk. Cardamom-laced chai already infuses in the fridge, to entice me later. (Loose tea leaves + water + jar + fridge = cold-brewed yum.) I sit, write, and turn in two short pieces to one client. I take a long phone interview for another. As with sugar, I expect withdrawal headaches. As with sugar, they don't come. I could use a midafternoon jolt to push through fatigue for a 7:00 p.m. interview. My body hurts as I fight it (especially as the interviewee forgets and has to push our talk until eight), and I am certainly not my sharpest . . . but at that hour, I wouldn't be even with caffeine. With only a little time winding down in bed after, I fall asleep fast. I sleep hard. Worsened headaches don't come the next day; but my normal headaches don't go away either. The night anxiety doesn't disappear—I still list Wonder Women and fade—but I sleep through the second night too. I fall asleep earlier the next.

Still . . . I'm not sure if uninhibited adenosine is worth it.

My mental energy is decent in the mornings. But it fades within three to five hours of putting foot to floor, and then disappears entirely midafternoon; windows often correlated with adrenal fatigue and blood sugar lows I try to normalize by eating regularly. It's hard to explain this kind of brain fog, but it's not just being tired. It's not even like how your head feels during the flu, so full of fluff you can't quite understand voices on the television, or remember why you have a pen or battery or brush in your hand, or that the word you want to say is "orange." It's even more than that. It's being unable to put words in order—a significant problem for someone who makes their living honing words. It's carrying around a heavy lead suit, one that hangs from the skin on your eyes and your skull and behind your kneecaps and your tailbone. As days pass, I Sherlock that my regular drops in late-morning mental energy are, indeed, a cause of my illness and not lack of coffee. (I've tackled this with naps, diet, vitamins, Eastern and Western medicine, fresh air; but one Challenge stone at a time.)

Accepting now that my brain has limited hours to do any serious writing, I try to better anticipate this quick-closing window. I wake even earlier, as I truly enjoy these morning hours. I first tackle projects that require the most creative part of my brain, keeping my in-box and social media feeds closed; this increases productivity of finishing actual stories. In the afternoon, I then check off things that drain less from both mind and body: I enjoy turning over spring clothes, walking Mitra, reading, or clearing out the waiting in-box. Prioritizing hard-to-hit work tasks first thing is a healthy habit not reserved for those with illness; many in high-achieving careers or leadership positions practice the same. I guess I just had to come to this structure in my own way.

By Challenge end, I'm excited to hop back on the coffee wagon.

And, also, a touch disappointed.

I conclude the mystery headaches that started in August aren't magically correlated with the caffeine I started drinking more of *later* that same year; if anything, the right amount of caffeine helps clear my pounding, foggy brain. (I also like having more than three or four highly focused work hours in a day.) But unlike loathing to give up my

No Sugar Challenge indulgences of brownies-in-bed, I would gladly trade coffee indefinitely for greater health. And aside from that, I rediscovered the joy of choosing black, green, white, or herbal tea moment to moment this week, having forced myself out of the habit of only reaching for the coffee pot.

How do I trust I'm not just telling myself this so to get back on the juice?

Similar to how a "little bit" of insulin is too hard to define for an individual, I read up that caffeine addiction is largely up to self-assessment: given what we observe and physically feel, do we suspect a problem? Can we identify physical symptom versus emotional anxiety? If we do suspect a problem, professional opinion suggests we cut down (not out) our intake and observe. We reduce and observe some more. We combine regular coffee with decaf. We drink more tea. And a lot more water.[109]

I already do these things.

I'm going to trust my ability to self-assess.

My self-self-help plan is looking smart from where I sip.

GOGGLEBOXED

No Television

A child is brought into a small room. They sit with a familiar researcher—someone they've played games with several times before and so trust. The researcher points the child's attention to a small marshmallow on a table. The researcher has to step out. The child may eat the marshmallow. But if they can wait a little while, the researcher will return and the child will get *two* marshmallows!

So goes the seminal Marshmallow Test.

In the study, begun in the 1960s by Walter Mischel at Stanford University's Bing Nursery School, researchers quantified the children who ate the marshmallow almost immediately, those who averaged three minutes before caving, and those who waited for the additional treat. (Pretzel or cookie, small toy or poker chip—the prize didn't matter.) Thirty years later, follow-up studies showed that the most self-controlled group averaged 210 points higher on their SATs[110] and a lower body mass index.[111]

Could success in life be so simply marshmallow-marked?

Thousands of adapted studies followed, pitting temptation against self-control. Some focused on coping mechanisms: How do we distract ourselves from giving in to temptation? When do we bother trying? Sometimes, Mischel notes, "willpower fatigue and plain old fatigue and exhaustion"[112] most lead us to fail. Other times, dark emotional scenarios have us choose shopping and sugar marshmallows over long-term growth.

Professor David thinks emotion can be used to our benefit.

Specifically, the emotion of gratitude.

In his case studies, he sent unsuspecting volunteers to perform arduous computer tasks. They then "almost lost" all progress made due to "computer failure" until "another test taker" came in to help and saved the work. This induced actual feelings of gratitude in the subjects. Then, their marshmallow: Would they take one hundred dollars in a year or a smaller amount now? (Real money.) Those reporting general happiness or neutrality averaged needing only eighteen dollars for present satisfaction. Those who felt grateful were more future-oriented. "They required thirty dollars now before forgoing the future one hundred dollar reward," Professor David noted. That makes for "a 12 percent increase, resulting only from a simple and fleeting nudge toward feeling grateful."[113]

Before my Year started, I'd peacocked on *Love Bites* that "I can do anything for forty days." I hadn't taken into account how loneliness would make going without social media a legit Challenge. Or how Election Night vulnerability would get me *thisclose* to drinking the proverbial marshmallow. My half-assed January attempt to reduce TV intake, indeed, failed when "plain old fatigue and exhaustion" justified a return to bingeing.

While no longer concerned that my relationships live only in my phone, I field a new fear that too much of my time falls to a gadget: the one mounted across from my bed. I need to mingle, to schmooze, to move from network television to real-life-networking. And I'm curious as to how my new mellow-yellow attitude will see space and silence when the screen stays black.

Four months from my first go, I'm feeling *happy, comma* gratitude.

It's time to go without television again.

For real. *Total without* this time.

The week starts easy. I work downtown, meet a colleague for a glass of wine, come home happily buzzed, and fall asleep before I get too far in a new Isabel Allende novel. Through the coming work days, I'm reminded how a lunch break with a book intellectually inspires far more than ogling Ted Mosby on *How I Met Your Mother* reruns. I tear through podcasts while folding laundry and organizing supplements. I fall asleep faster without endless streaming.

Then, the week goes on. Temptation builds.

Wednesday, I work a long food story day, interviewing on site in a restaurant and then staying late to dine with Dearie Darling Friend Erin. I sleep hard but am overtired the next day; the bed-and-TV combo wails like a siren. I fight for productivity and by noon contemplate cheating. I don't. Instead, I scare myself straight by researching TV consumption statistics and then race to bed petrified, feeling like

I've watched every episode of Black Mirror at once. I resist the cheat urge Friday, too, first from my desk and then the reading chair: I layer blankets, pour tea, and fall into Allende. After our Riverside Writers meeting Saturday, I read until the novel is done.

I crave a Sunday of bed and bingeing.

Instead, I put on a yellow sweater.

I slap on minimal makeup.

I pull up my ovaries.

I head downtown.

I enter an upscale restaurant and wind to the private dining room, packed to the brim with pastry chefs and food writer folk. I hug friends. I laugh! I meet lovely new humans. I smile. I swap cards and talk potential stories. *This is good*, I remind myself. I feel *happy, comma* for ninety minutes, then drag home.

I listen to jazz on public radio while dinner sautés.

My joints creak. My head throbs.

Night falls, and with it, I finally fall into bed.

I just *can't* anymore.

"Oy, with the poodles already." All right, Lorelais. You win.

I cave.

According to a recent Nielsen report, adults my age average four-and-a-half hours a day of watching television live, DVRd, or app-streamed.[114] (Many households don't have television while others watch nonstop, so that number pulls widely ranging groups to the middle.) As Designer-Amber articulated, devices make us easy habitual consumers: DVRs hoard, and apps continually stream. That Nielsen report records a key milestone: for the first time in history, "availability of SVoD (subscription video on demand) programming (Netflix, Hulu Plus, Amazon Prime) is now equal to DVR penetration, with both available in 50 percent of US TV households." We don't even have to own a membership; sharing login info allows digital libraries to jump households.

This week, TV-free time reminded me of the glories of the luscious novel. I fell asleep faster. I was more tush-pushed to sip Chardonnay with colleagues on a spring afternoon.

All good things, yes.

Still, I struggled to exert will over a one-week absence.

This bothers me.

Is this a matter of the *value* of the proverbial marshmallow?

Or have I again discovered a health cost *need* versus a want?

Or am I not yet where gratitude makes the "marshmallow" a nonissue?

I ask Professor David about manipulated emotions. He's both put test subjects in such scenarios of gratitude and also had them only reflect upon situations for which they felt thankful. "We'll get the same result, in terms of adult versions of the Marshmallow Test," he tells me.

I started this Year ineffectually counting blessings.

What am I missing? Where's the action that makes this difference?

"If you're just doing the list, filling it out like you'd write your name on a tax form, it's not going to do anything," he explains. "If you actually take the time to visualize—let yourself simulate it in your mind and feel what you were feeling—then it will. It's about doing these things in a way that actually evokes the emotion versus just going through the motions."

"So it really is that simple?"

"It's that simple."

"Wonderful!"

"All you have to do is reinstantiate the feeling. Five or ten minutes a day are enough . . . If you're motivated to find and cultivate little habits—to cultivate those emotions—they'll do the same thing."

Looking back, I realize my counting blessings probably resembled a disenchanted Natalie Wood in *Miracle on 34th Street*: "I believe, I believe. It's silly, but I believe . . ." I wasn't visualizing or simulating scenarios of thanks. I wasn't savoring past experiences.

I think there's something to be said for evoking gratitude not only for the past, but for the present too. Rather than lingering on the *why* of this TV habit, what might happen if I just embrace it instead? If I stop thinking of it as a bad thing and accept that the screen brings me joy *if* I don't just endlessly stream or "go through the motions"? If I savor this pleasure while it's happening, might positive neurons fire-and-wire? Might long-term happiness grow?

And from the flat screen, where to next?

If I stop and savor the writing process that often intimidates me rather than worrying about pitches and editors, will my work infuse with greater joy?

If I stop and savor social mixers instead of fixating on how I look or my low energy, will those relationships become even more fun and loving?

If I stop and savor the light falling into my bedroom as I read *or* watch television *or* work, will I sleep more soundly at night?

Will savoring bring me a more bountiful future reward?

I don't know.

But I'm going to have fun waiting for the marshmallows.

PANTSED

No Comfy Clothes

Karl Lagerfeld once told *Vogue* readers, "Sweatpants are a sign of defeat. You lost control of your life, so you bought some sweatpants."[115]

I took control of my life when I shifted careers to work from home. Working in sweatpants is my prize.

But have I let my love for leggings go too far?

I have no problem putting together a casual-cute ensemble. But anything someone my age would wear in a professional position? Catastrophe. Could this play into my major confidence question? For this mini-Challenge, I'll be office attire–ready before 9:00 a.m. I will not change outfits if going out for the evening, as I'd have to do if going to an office daily. I'll relax a touch on the weekend but still gloss up a bit more than my norm.

What will fortify if I put more effort into my aesthetic?

Will the scaffolding around my morning time management shift?

Will a more polished look affect my sense of self?

Will I have more confidence in my work?

Less imposter syndrome in communication?

Will going without sweatpants fix everything, Karl?!

Day One, I regret this stupid idea.

Awake by seven and exhausted from yesterday's pastry party, I don't have the energy to shower. I brush things and cycle through three outfits before settling on slim jeans and a black sweater I plan to dress up for a later event with heels and a blazer. I put on foundation and mascara and don't feel my brain's any more qualified to work. Eight hours later, humidity breaks my stay-in-these-clothes willpower: jeans to a packed walk-around event? Hell no. Yes, if at an office, I'd have to wear what I've got on. But *I'm not in an office, Karl.* I cheat. I change. Five times. I settle on a dress. I reapply melted makeup. I leave late, but I look good.

Tuesday, I wake to a body hurting.

I cheat again. But this time with Internet support.

In a story on *The Tylt*, 68.5 percent of readers vote that #LeggingsArePants![116] *Bustle* writer Erin McKelle points out that *Merriam-Webster's* supports the classification, defining pants as "an outer garment covering each leg separately and usually extending from the waist to the ankle," and she personally doesn't "want to have my outfit choices philosophized unto by you or anyone else . . ."[117] (I like this McKelle person.)

Within a sphere that feels Challenge-fair, I dress as if heading to a *Love Bites* recording, layering leggings, knee socks, fitted shirts, and sweaters. I put on makeup. I exert *effort*. I also accept that comfort has become my MO for a reason: softness soothes. "Comfort should absolutely be one of the first rules of style, and I refuse not to wear a piece of clothing because it's comfortable—isn't that sort of masochistic?" my new BFF Leggings McKelle opines.

Wednesday morning, I try and fail to make a pair of office-appropriate, deep-blue, wide-legged pants look cool and casual. The cashmere sweater I pair with them is not *right*, and instead of feeling artsy and urban I feel like the frazzled-mom-of-a-second-grader. (No offense, second-grade moms. I just assume you're even more tired than I, and this outfit looks *tired*.) It's weird-humid again. The cashmere sticks. By eight, I slip back into skinny jeans and a white button-down and decide I need to hit the thrift scene and buy pants.

And if I want to feel put together in the mornings, I need to shower.

Thursday, I'm clean by seven thirty. I blow-dry my hair and slip on a maxi dress. (Sweatpants in dress form!) I swipe on makeup and put on jewelry. I walk taller, move sassier. Friday: skinny jeans, comfy top, makeup, done. Saturday: I put on an old sleeveless jumper and a light sweater for a relaxing day out with a friend, but *blegh* hair makes me ponder a cut. (Maybe I should take better care of my hair in general?) Sunday: a leggings-top-sweater combo, a thin sheen of makeup, and clipped hair all happen before an early walk.

As we trace the Hudson, I gleefully declare:

I'm thirty-five and can wear what I want!

I'm single and can do what I want!

I'm a work-from-home freelancer, so I can work in what I want!

I like the ageless age I am!

But still . . . This week, I wasted too much energy in an area of life begging for improvement. Like reworking my old fear of disposability, this is not a new conundrum; I've recognized for a long while that the more insecure I feel, the more I hide behind clothing: I wear black, I disregard shape, and I don't invest in new items. Happy-Home Rebecca believes clothes should have purpose. "I often dress in really bright clothes," she says. "Both because I love them and they make me smile, but also because when I go to a networking event, my clothes do half the work for me. People are like, 'Oh, I love your skirt!' They approach me, instead of me having to do all the work. I'm putting my clothes . . . to work for me. That's what makes them right or wrong."

I've not bought new pants since losing weight.

I've not recently gotten a haircut.

I move hangers down the line and am bored by what I see.

I am so far from right, right now.

It's time to buckle down.

To costume the toolkit of a dreamier, braver, badass businesswoman.

But at home?

I'm back in sweatpants.

Sorry, Karl. (Nah. Totally not sorry.)

CUT OFF

No Working Past 5:00 p.m.

I pick three favorite inherited traits from both of my parents.

From my mother: assumption of goodness in others; an instinct to pitch in and help; and a delight in simple pleasures like a walk by the ocean or hours with a good book. From my father: an open-door policy that welcomes all to the table; a knack for turning even a short trip into an adventure; and a work ethic that gives purpose to every sunrise.

That last one is a double-edged sword.

There's a word in Japanese for overworking to literal death: *karōshi*. Post–World War II, the decimated country rebuilt into one of today's largest world economies at a grave cost: overworked citizens as young as their twenties increasingly committed suicide and died from heart failure, stroke, and other illness. By the 1970s, researchers labeled such work-related death *karōshi*: "overwork death."[118] In a culture of nonrefusal—where workers are also parents, partners, and friends—eventually, the body can do no more. It gives out. [119]

Save Japan and Korea, Americans work the most hours of any advanced economy. And we excel in another realm defined by the Japanese: *furoshiki* ("cloaked overtime"). We average more fifty-plus-hour workweeks than other advanced economies, then work more out-of-office hours too. Yet for all this *furoshiki*, countries like France and Denmark surpass us in hourly productivity. In fact, working longer hours in those countries is considered job *inefficiency*.[120]

I once felt great pride in my inherited overwork ethic. For a period of time when Ruark and I lived together, I worked two day jobs, starred in one theater show at night, and stayed up late sewing costumes for another. We watched a lot of *Family Guy* back then, laughing at the cartoon family headed up by Peter and Lois Griffin. One day:

"Peter, are you sure Santos and Pasqual don't mind coming in on a Saturday to serve us drinks?"

"Are you kidding, Lois? They're Portuguese. Work is their cocaine."[121]

Ruark ~~melodramatically~~ guffawed at this exchange.

He knew work was my unhealthy fix.

I fell severely sick again less than a year later.

After my parents separated, Dad and I eventually discussed the pressures of his working to provide for our large family; Mom and I, how his constant workload affected all our lives. Then he had open-heart surgery in 2015 to replace a valve that had been slowly leaking since birth. We've since examined our struggles against restriction: our ambitions (or egos?) drive us forward while our bodies slow us down.

The final week of this Challenge, I contemplate this collective hurricane.

Can I work more efficiently?

Will greater time management foster financial prosperity?

Moderation offer calmer health?

I remove the option of working past 5:00 p m

Monday, I do production work for *Love Bites*. I lose out financially in this job; so it goes for podcasts on independent stations without massive sponsorship. But I think I'm efficient in this passion project? And working in this medium strengthens my network, broadens my skill set, and expands my audience—areas I assume pay me back elsewhere. I schedule a recording, pull research, formulate questions, and work on website content. I enjoy this work. But the clock runs faster than I anticipate. I need to write a feature print story for a food client I love who also pays well; an uncommon duo. I don't get far in this before 5:00 p.m. hits.

I vow to better prioritize Tuesday.

I start that story first thing. But then a decently paying podcast client offers potential last-minute work. I can't say "no" when work comes in. I just *can't*. I shift my attention to frantically pulling research and scheduling interviews. I live up to what I say I can accomplish in their short window, but their side proves erratic. The story drops. I've lost most of the day. It's four thirty when a third client's revision request comes in, and now I'm frazzled from hopping around. I open the document to see *major* red-pennage on my submission. I take a deep, deep, *deep* breath. It's our first time working together; apparently, there was a huge disconnect between the kind of stories they thought I write and the style I thought they wanted.

I wash with relief when the clock strikes five—I can't obsess over failure.

In my corner chair with book and tea, I ponder:

Two days, four clients, nothing submitted.

No paycheck makes its way toward my mailbox.

I'm getting in my own way.

I have to work smarter.

Wednesday, I schedule follow-up interviews for the bombed print piece.

Then I write, edit, submit, and invoice the big print one.

Copper boom!

Thursday, I work the job boards.

I want to feel smug disgust for Rory's complete ineptitude at pursuing work. But (a) Schadenfreude has never been my thing, and (b) I've been there: one minute, a small roster of clients steadily assigns and pays you, and then seemingly overnight you have no work. I was hypothetically tap-dancing at 2:00 a.m. before I realized how drastically my client list had shrunk from regular columns to irregular features (better paid, harder to land, longer to execute) and my pitch list seemed never-ending.

I need more new consistent clients.

I apply for a part-time interviewer job with a company that writes biographies; with over three hundred chats under my belt, I am more than equipped for this gig. I submit a résumé and clips to a site needing short bios done of chefs and caterers; another obvious fit. I pass a third's writing test with flying colors. They all require slightly different submissions; slightly varying résumés; different samples. It's a lot of concentration, and 5:00 p.m. can't come soon enough.

(I never hear back from the first two. I don't get hired for the third.)

Friday, I update my LinkedIn profile, make a portfolio on yet another site for freelancers, and scan the job boards now long bookmarked on my browser.

I take a look at the revision request again.

I hope this new client and I find a happy medium.

I am so, so out of money.

I need to land some big work and soon.

Two weeks ago, Sarah Robb O'Hagan came on to *Love Bites*. A powerhouse CEO who worked for Gatorade and Equinox before writing her book *Extreme You: Step Up. Stand Out. Kick Ass. Repeat,* Sarah guides readers into rising from failure, making brave decisions, and living large. Of course, I asked her on to discuss moderation: How do we *not* say "yes" to every opportunity that comes our way out of fear for making the wrong choice? "Saying 'no' is important to do when you're just not fucking feeling it!" she'd shared. The right job is a magic mix of opportunity, people, and work culture. "Not all of it's going to add up perfectly, but your gut's gonna scream at you if it's feeling right. I think that's a good one to listen to," she said.[122]

Ben then contributed his three-point system of consideration for taking a gig: Will the job fulfill creatively? Will it potentially advance his career? Will the money be good? Only if two of three answers are *yes* will he take the job.

I consider this past week's workload from these angles.

At the top of the Year, I'd stopped trusting my gut's reaction for good reason: I'd said "yes" to too many people and projects that failed to produce financial, creative, or career growth. While I'm stripping away Band-Aids and exposing an instinct I hope will serve me better, I don't trust it . . . yet. So I apply Ben's three-point system to this past week's clients.

Love Bites fulfills me creatively and in some ways advances my career. But I lose a lot of money in the time devoted to it, the scales tipping in a way that my growing skill set, network, and audience don't yet financially tip back. The new print and other podcast client both pay well. But they don't significantly affect my career projection. And unless we better get on the same page, I'll find neither creatively fulfilling and lose time that makes their paycheck insubstantial. With the feature food client, I get it all: I love the team I work for and the stories I get to work on, and my editors compensate me respectfully. I need to prioritize them, always.

Then, there's what I got back, shutting my laptop at 5:00 p.m.

I had more time to revel in sunset walks and books. To leisurely tend my home. To soak in the bath and laze on the yoga mat. To think through the stories I wanted to write and the conversations I needed to have.

Shouldn't I factor calm restoration in my decision-making process too?

As the workweek wraps, all I am sure of is that for the near future I'll trade career advancement for a stable bank account. I can get by with less creative satisfaction in my work if it makes room for pleasure time with family. For road trips with friends. For walks in the woods. For maybe something or someone entirely new.

I might have accomplished less work in quantity this week. But I'm pretty sure my efficiency is building toward something healthier. Something I hope on the path toward a work–life balance more in line with my greater purpose.

Something akin to what the Japanese call *ikigai*: a reason for being.

That's a word I could embrace, no matter the time of day.

I have a feeling both my parents could get on board with that.

QUITTING TIME

PHYSICAL BODY: Anything that helps me sleep better or feel more comfortable at my desk increases my productivity. And I have a feeling the less time I *force* my body to sit and work, the healthier it will be and the more efficient my time working.

SOCIAL INTERACTIONS: I work with amazing people; I want to wear a confident costume when out and about with them. I want to meet more of them, so we can joyfully interact and craft more stories together.

SENSE OF SELF: With reset scales, I plan to better choose jobs that fulfill needs I want met. I'll spend less time weighing job decisions and, I hope, move forward with greater clarity and confidence.

***

Spoiler alert: Rory Gilmore starts writing a memoir, *The Gilmore Girls*.

She makes it look easy. "I sat down last night and outlined the first five chapters, just like that," she tells her mother. "That's a sign . . . that this is it. This is what I'm supposed to do." She writes in the empty silence of her grandparents' manicured mansion, pages flying. Yes, I'm *jealous*. Because despite the lack of work ethic I've watched on screen for hours now, I assume fictional Rory is still a far superior writer than real-life me (#ImposterSyndrome). I also trust that, in golden cinematic glory, her memoir will be a best-selling success.

Yet here I am, stranger than fiction, acquiescing that there is no clear path for any freelance creative: no time card, dress code, social norm, or set precedents for behavior guaranteeing the next gig or big paycheck. It's a rough road for all of us. Rory had to find hers, just as I have to find mine.

There's relief in this lesson.

When I was a young theater student, I presumed there was a "correct" way to play a part; I'd observe actors who sort of looked like me in the roles I wanted and emulate their work. My art was, therefore, safe. After I presented one of my very favorite Shakespearean scenes, the professor stared up at our mock-stage for a long while. Then he slowly nodded and said: "Well, that was right. It was boring. But it was right." I was crushed. Few pushed me from this comfort zone. It took experience and maturity to eventually build up my artistic bravery.

Then again, at the start of this Year, I admitted to hiding behind interviews in a similar way.

Now, I feel a bit more motivation to express fully.

In my current state of physical limitation, I can't execute everything I want to accomplish in a day. But restructuring this week, I better understand how all of us only get one lifetime in which to achieve anything. Time passes quickly. We can choose how we fill it and choose to take out the things that don't serve us well.

I don't want to work hard and play harder.

I want to savor every gentle bit of the work and play I get.

But still, I'm jealous of Rory. At the end of this Challenge, I see no clear signs propelling me toward "this is what I'm supposed to do." Do I put writing aside for more financially lucrative work? Or keep hounding the job boards? What other jobs can I do in this body? With these skills? I intentionally took on four small Challenges to shake up the larger picture. But now I'm only left with more air in which to breathe possibility. To ponder questions. To recognize *have* and *could be*.

I can work. I can abstain. I can observe.

I guess I'll just keep asking questions.

I'll keep on the path to finding myself.

CHAPTER
CHALLENGE **9**

MULTIPLE CHALLENGE TWO!

CHALLENGE: Multiple Challenge!

TIME LINE: Four days

RULES: All past Challenges at once—again!

Soaking in the tub, I rewatch the *Gilmore Girls* revival. (I admit it: I'm addicted.)

Upon second viewing, it's Lorelai's mature but unsure lack of direction that slays me. "Suddenly, I feel like I'm standing still. Like the whole world is moving . . . and I'm standing completely still," she says.

Nearing the end of my Year, I find myself in the center of my own tornado, not knowing what move to make next. Should I change careers? Do I now enjoy not dating so much that I want to stay single indefinitely? If every fulfilled "future self" I meet in meditation lives in an isolated woodland home, should I actively plan a move toward that future?

I hope four Multiple Challenge days will slow swirling thoughts.

En route home from an interview, I find myself without a want to *do* something. (This happens naturally now. And often.) I haven't brought a book. I don't gravitate to a podcast. I can't scroll social. I sit. I think.

What do I need right now? Thoughts organize.

I scratch words in my Moleskin, sketching long-term to-do lists and typing short-term e-mails as the train races north. As I think and list, I feel increasingly focused, energized, and present. I make chips in what have lately felt like uncarvable boulders. Walking the final steps home, I marvel at how asking myself such a simple question could create space to get so much done.

Back at my desk, a quick in-box scan shows an e-mail I don't want to read—I'm almost positive it's a significant work rejection that will send me down an emotional, self-sabotaging spiral. Before-Year-me would open it immediately.

I do not.

I sit in my corner chair. I read my book.

I slowly sip my coffee. (*Dammit.* I'm not supposed to drink coffee.)

After fifteen minutes, I take the empty cup into the kitchen.

I set a two-minute timer. I stand at the window.

I Wonder Woman. I Wonder Women.

What do I need right now?

Not falling back into old habits requires me to ask this question constantly.

Sunlight streams through budding trees to warm my face. Birds chirp the bliss of spring. I press my feet against the floor. I breathe. The sentence shifts: I *have everything* I *need right now.* I have food, a safe home, and work. I have a sunny day and soft clothes and quiet. I have love and friendship.

Shit. Professor David was right.

I'm not listing. I'm *feeling.*

This works.

I go back to my desk. I read the e-mail and it stings, so I put it aside to address later when better ready. I continue tackling to-dos. Executing this twenty-minute process saves the rest of a day that, only a few months ago, would have been lost to anxiety and grief.

hab·it: a settled or regular tendency or practice, especially one that is hard to give up.[123]

And I still have Forty Final days of giving up to do.

CHAPTER
CHALLENGE **10**

NO HABIT

CHALLENGE: In a final quest to forge my own path, I will shift one habit daily, from something as simple as brushing my teeth with my nondominant hand to as Challenging as going entirely without technology.

TIME LINE: Forty days

RULES: Take out habit. One Day apiece. Observe. Record. Move on.

WONT

On June 20, 2016, I stepped out on a forty-day path.

Then My Year, Without took direction.

But it never set me toward a fixed destination.

I'm not sure where these Final Forty days will leave me.

As the one simple study of social media transformed into self-self-help, I've increasingly sought guidance from books, documentaries, TED Talks, podcasts, formal interviews, and casual conversation. I've watched Roko's *Happy* more than once since first viewing it a few months ago; when struggling, I'll put it on and smile at Okinawan centenarians or a Louisiana Basin nature lover. *Happy* is also where I either first found or remet some of the psychologists whose work I've explored during this journey, like Dr. Happiness Ed Diener's subjective well-being, Tim Kasser's analysis of the hedonic treadmill, Daniel Gilbert's hilarious *Stumbling Upon Happiness*, and Sonja Lyubomirsky's thoughts on holiday presence. Unlike with other resources, I never reach out to these people, ignoring my journalistic reflex and allowing myself to be human while I slowly learn. Self-discovery is messy. My personal conclusions sometimes contradict their professional findings. Their analytics often feel like an entire tarot deck thrown into my lap—it takes time to sort the cards and apply them to my path.

I'm particularly curious about a few cards stuck to me.

In *Happy*, Lyubomirsky shares that 50 percent of our perception of happiness is genetically predetermined. Then, 10 percent is affected by circumstances like health and wealth. That leaves 40 percent neurologically up for the taking.

I've examined my inherited traits.

My health and wealth have not shifted.

But that remaining 40 percent?

Month after month, I feel it stretching in my brain.

I read it in books from my corner chair, while e-mails go unanswered. I ponder it in the sky while swinging in my hammock without agenda. I feel it in the smile I project to friends and colleagues, one that grows wider every day. I hear it in the inner monologue that continually shifts to a softer dialogue.

I can't expect indefinite *happy, comma* just yet though.

I want to use these Final Forty days to make sure my growth continues beyond this Year. But a body of research shows that we revert to a base level of happiness rather quickly after both extended periods of happiness-building and instances of trauma.[124] (There are, of course, exceptions to these.)

In one such extensive study, Lyubomirsky put (rigorously examined) test subjects through various activities traditionally associated with a greater sense of professed well-being, then assessed them with (industry-approved) analytical methods and measured them against control groups. "First and foremost," she concluded of those who succeeded in achieving greater happiness, "people need both a will and a proper way."[125] Just like my lack of want had me fail at abstaining from television, she first found that only those truly invested in the activities and motivated for change would progress. Then, the self-improvement methods they practiced needed to be legit; proverbial placebos didn't change anything in their happiness wiring.

Most relevant to my final Challenge, Lyubomirsky found that we so quickly adapt to routine that if we don't switch up happiness activities, we revert to baseline happiness. Our brain is so good at acting without our engagement that many routines we complete daily can be viewed as habit: the ways in which we walk, sit, or stand; how we type; how we brush our teeth and hair; which brands we buy; how we rise from bed; our patterns of locking the house and turning on the car, etc. We run through these tasks so often that they require almost no active thought. Considered separately, changing up something as small as in which hand I hold Mitra's leash might seem an insignificant Challenge. But in *Happy*, Lyubomirsky says even changing a running route makes a huge difference in our happiness-building—that's why we do such things at the gym or by trying a new hobby. The brain just needs to be engaged.

Final Forty days. Forty percent of the brain.

One percent a day? One habit a day?

Yes. I'll change one small habit daily, jotting down the shift and observations. Reflecting upon my "experience of the experience" (as Gilbert defines *awareness*), I'll attempt to push myself out of mindless routine entirely.

In *The Power of Habit*, Journalist-Duhigg emphasizes that a failure backup plan is often the difference between the person who gives up and the person who rises and presses on. To make sure I never find myself waking without a habit to change, I start a list of things I may or may not attempt:

- One Day of not apologizing for anything
- One Day of not carrying a purse (How do men do it?)
- One Day of no talking—not even to Mitra
- One Day of not looking in mirrors
- One Day of not cleaning up after myself
- One Day of no electricity (Go easy, make it a weekend.)
- One Night of no pajamas (Sleep naked. Because I can.)
- One Day of waking to a self-motivation audio track— like my spirit friend Frankie Bergstein of *Grace and Frankie*—instead of an alarm on my phone
- One Day of wearing a *totally not me* outfit—in public
- One Day of Yes (to things I want to say "no" to, à la Shonda Rhimes)

I keep scribbling, listing ideas contributed by friends, byproducts of random articles, and weird combinations of thought fragments and Fraggle-like creativity. I get twenty or so down before I stop and take this all in.

I'm a long way from where I started.

This is no longer about seeking a relationship, health, or wealth.

This is simply about living every percent of these Final Forty days.

CONNECTEDNESS

(Social Interactions)

I click down a Brooklyn sidewalk.

Again, the heroine of a clichéd movie scene.

This time, though, it's not a wine-dripped rom-com.

It's the night before my Final Forty days begin. Far from Roberta's backyard and one Year later, I'm again wearing my salvaged seventies skirt and flowered tank. I'm headed to another evening with radio folk; this time, a storytelling event hosted by The Listening Booth, which produces Julia's *The Lonely Hour*. I walk in and, again, immediately flush. Julia and I have never met in person. I don't recognize a face among the sharply dressed, creative crowd. But I'm not flushing social fear. My skin only pinks from a typical hour spent traversing the steamy New York City transit system and the adrenaline needed to trek down in a pained body that asked me to stay home.

I want to be here. I just don't feel social.

A Multiple Challenge day; I can't fall into my phone or drink.

This is all okay.

I weave around the massive space. I smile and nod to humans clustered—no one beckons me into conversation, and I don't push. I get a seltzer from the bar and take in how the light bounces off the Gowanus Bay. Deep armchairs look deliciously inviting; how content I would be to sink and enjoy the paperback *Anne of Ingleside* burning a hole in my purse. I do feel slightly awkward. But not because of how

I stand separate and don't even pretend to be busy; more in that I wish it was socially acceptable to sit and read, alone among others.

What is a need?

In the No Shopping Challenge, I defined a *need* as food, water, shelter, etc. The supersmart human crew expands that such securities are but one of four *psychological needs*. Treadmill-Kasser classifies that "a need, in the sense used here, is not just something a person desires or wants, but is something that is necessary to his or her survival, growth, and optimal functioning."[126] This Year, I've inadvertently explored areas around all four psychological need groups: 1) I've reexamined the wealth and material needs that bring *safety, security,* and *sustenance.* 2) My Challenge sense-of-self meter correlates with *competence, efficacy,* and *self-esteem.* 3) Considering my social interactions, I study *connectedness.* 4) And weighing my physical health against my human value, I explore my *autonomy* and *authenticity.*

Moving from Multiple Challenge into Final Forty, I ponder *connectedness.*

"Humans strongly desire intimacy and closeness with others, going to great lengths to seek out and secure such relationships," Treadmill-Kasser says. In one study, Dr. Happiness Diener discovered that committed, interactive relationships were most vital in the happiest 10 percent of case subjects.[127] Happy-Home Rebecca stresses the value of energy going into relationships over objects. Loneliness-Cacioppo points out even the most isolated can be happy if professing strong social ties.

On that first *Love Bites* episode, I'd professed frustration with *dis*connection; most of my relationships felt lived out in my phone. Turning off Anthropologist-Amber's "panic architecture," I learned how to reassess what I most need from human connection. I never robustly returned to Facebook or Twitter. I now approach Instagram in a way that feels progressively truer to who I am: a bit dreamy, vulnerably honest, and playfully curious. Though I spend even more time ill and alone now, I feel less lonely than I ever have before. "Isolation is not an objective concept," Happy-Roko and I discuss, trying to better understand my shift. "If you're forced into isolation because of an illness, I guess the lesson from the research is to figure out a way to maintain your relationships regardless."

Life is hard. We all struggle.

And relationships are living, breathing things.

Vulnerability takes long-term commitment, patience, and trust. We don't know how someone else will react to our words or how we'll then react to their response, in live conversation, everyone's taking the gamble. Separation and the fickleness of technology can make combining worlds even more difficult. Only after I learned what *doesn't* work for me could I creatively embrace technology as a tool to help strengthen my relationships.

My sisters live far away: Big Sis in Indiana, Lil' Sis in North Carolina. For a while, I struggled to articulate this current wave of illness to them. I worried this doubled division was weakening our bonds. Learning from the increased quiet, I started asking them for "movie nights": we pick a movie on an app we all have access to, time our screens together, and hit Play. We text or FaceTime as we watch, discussing nothing of importance, commenting as if together. The regularly shared time invites greater relationship responsibility on both sides; I feel less nervous about calling them when in emotional need; I hope they better trust I'm there to support their struggles too.

FW Lyndsey lives in Virginia. Almost every morning, I audio record a chapter of a book for her while sipping my coffee. She then listens during her breakfast and audio records thoughts back. We started with passages of Henry David Thoreau's journals—a weathered copy of *Winter* gave us the daily "we go deep" nature joy we both seek—then moved on to other books of magical realism. This system of voice memo app and text message helps us keep up a conversation separate from those around our respective struggles with our bodies.

SW Rose lives in California. She has a busy teaching schedule and I go to bed early, so exchanges come mostly by written word: I read her book recommendations, and she shares classroom lesson plans. In the New Year, I struggle to type the sample chapter, sick in bed; while I sleep, she reads pages, sends suggestions, and becomes one of my most sharp-eyed editors. This starts a regular exchange of life updates, and an old friend feels closer every day.

Such small shifts this Year have been my everything.

Day One, I wonder how my morning might change if I spend physical time around other humans, instead of alone.

I step foot in the coffee shop by seven fifteen. I'm surprised to find it so quiet, so completely unlike the bustle of a packed Sunday crowd. I chat with the women behind the counter, take my Americano, and sit. *What a different scene than that from my desk, only a block away!* Light bounces freely off of old buildings that line the wide street; I see it through a wall of windows, so different from how my narrow desk-view opens only to light mischievously winding its way around iron railings and on to brick. The shop doors open and shut. I hear buses pass, one voice call to another, a truck engine kick in, all mingling with Sam Cooke's voice dancing from overhead speakers—all a whir so different from the punctuated blast of street sound that startles through my silence at home.

Frazzled parents enter with children crying for cinnamon buns they're not given. Commuters in suits and worn black sneakers come in and go out again. Tables start to fill. I frequently make eye contact. I smile at strangers. There's the occasional quick chat. I'm connected to this scene—to the light, the sound, the movement, and the living people. Here, the social system is built in; I'm welcomed and accepted, a woman alone with her work.

Interacting with strangers this morning feels "right."

Wandering solo at last night's storytelling event felt "right" too.

I am now fully in love with being one singular human person.

I know my relationships—my very real loved ones, the literary figures I cleave to, and the cheerleading voices in my head—are always with me.

They come with me as Days of the Final Forty move on.

One Day, I go without a purse to dinner with a friend, holding keys, phone, and credit card in deep dress pockets. Without stuff distracting, I sit fully present on the subway. Then, within the ambiance of the restaurant as I wait. And then again, with even more focused vulnerability in our open heart-to-heart.

One Day, I have to "give one or go without one." I've started a new phase of self-exploration in my relationship with money, trying to figure out: Why do I emotionally rebel against having any? Why do I feel guilt at having a dollar more than the person next to me? Does my going further into debt help anyone? Does my inability to sustain myself contribute to society at large? How do I even *feel* in the moment of giving? To face this small piece of the large pie, I set off in the day, promising to buy a stranger a cup of coffee or movie ticket before I get that same treat. The lesson comes easy: I enter the subway, and a neighbor needs a ride. I swipe him in, then me. We exchange a nod, two humans connected by a fulfilled need to get from A to B. I'll never see him again, and it's only a three-dollar lesson. I don't know where this fits into my bigger money picture. But it feels helpful? I think of FW Lyndsey's "It's something I can do." I can't do much right now. But I can throw this small stone of connectedness.

One Day, I "go without going." I usually feel extreme guilt when backing out of something I say I'll do because of illness. But when too sick to make it to a Suffering the Silence event, I make my last-minute absence my *without*. Specifically, I change the habit of guilt surrounding it. I tell myself: *You're not letting the world down by not going, Jacqueline.* I make myself *feel* this. I savor my bed and flat-screen streaming *Sunset Boulevard*. I remind myself of the trust lesson from the No Shopping Challenge: "My loved ones will still love me . . ."

One Day, I "go without a morning walking routine," eschewing the path Mitra and I normally tread so to intentionally meet new dogs (and their humans). We wind unfamiliar paths, and I'm reminded of just how many new people there are to meet, even this close to my home.

As the Year winds down and these One Day *withouts* have me pondering my place among other people, I'm again left with more questions than answers. I now feel stronger in solitude but better understand how relationships are more vital to my happiness than anything else. I yearn for a quiet rural life but know too much isolation isn't healthy for me. I now truly enjoy not dating and treasure single-gal independence, but also hold out hope that someone else out there might also enjoy this weird path I'm walking.

How long will I stay in this *question-mark-comma* place?

The alchemic mystery of this Year had me walk to the coffee shop on May 12, 2017—Day One of this Challenge. There, I found another sandwich board sign covered with pastel chalk words. Spelling out, plain as day:

"If it doesn't challenge you, it won't change you."

I think I'll be okay if my path doesn't come to an end on June 21, 2017. I've still got some challenging changing to do.

SELF-ESTEEM

(Sense of Self)

For One Day, I go without seeing my physical reflection.

Before bed, I cover my vanity mirror with a cloth napkin. I take down the one hanging from my closet door. I tuck a towel around the medicine cabinet and fold down my jewelry box. When I wake, I have no idea how puffy my morning skin looks. But brush bristles meeting my scalp feel *so satisfying*. I'm shocked at how many times I'd normally glance at my image: whenever I use the toilet; the dozens of times I pass through hall to kitchen; the open vanity reflecting my midsection as I cross the room. I don't have to leave my neighborhood today and so this doesn't much Challenge how I look in public. But taking pause to enjoy the softness of fleece in my leggings or the melt of lotion on my steaming skin after a bath, I'm more present in the body I project out of.

The next morning I groggily work in reverse, uncovering and taking down cloths as I brew coffee and get ready to walk. I put my hair—grungy from the bath—up in a knot. I enjoy textures as I dress. Then I pass a mirror and catch my reflection. I take down the hair and smooth it under a (soft, worn) wool cap. I cover tired skin with big sunglasses.

I probably didn't look great on my One Day without outer reflection.

I don't care.

One Day, I go without makeup. With a live *Love Bites* show on the docket, I'll face hordes of strangers on the subways, potentially run into people I know, see Ben and Engineer David, and meet the day's guest—all without a swipe of anything glamming my face. I can't overcompensate in ensemble—the contrast would be too harsh—

so I go for subtlety, layering sweaters and jewelry and tousling my hair with a little more "out of bed" volume than my norm. I click the sidewalks with genuine devil-may-care moxie. I meet the guest and command my mic, unashamed in my bare skin.

A few days later, I test the opposite.

I'm down about fifteen pounds from when I started taking notice in November. I've lost puff and gained confidence. But I'm wary of lessons learned from past experience; when some people see me *thinner*, they assume I'm *better*. From what I've learned from the supersmart human crew, I deduce that this is a psychological instinct to correlate thinness with success; they assume I must be feeling healthier than when we last met, right? No. I'm just . . . smaller. Or wearing makeup. Or trying *not* to look like a (nonexistent) textbook vision of a "sick person." Their snap-judgment appeases their conscience (as in, they've done the good deed of checking in), and I white-lie so to not insult the intentions I believe are genuinely kind.

But if I truly care about connectedness—if I want to increase my confidence and better advocate for others with illness—then I must figure out how to present *the honest me* amid the battle of "this is how my body *looks*" versus "this is how my body *feels*."

I don't want to use my skin as a suit for only *look* or *feel*.

Neither as a cloak of victory, nor as a mask.

For One Night, I vow to wear neither.

I make it hard for myself: I'm attending another work pastry shindig where I'm sure to see chefs and other writers I know. I dress up. I look good. But my body fights pain and fatigue. I will be honest when asked about anything.

I see my Delightful Friend Philip as I walk in. He compliments how I look but also asks about my health (#TrueFriends). I don't sugarcoat. A pastry colleague with Crohn's disease notes the weight loss and asks if it's healthy or not; I tell him I'm not great physically, but emotionally I've never been stronger. When a new acquaintance makes a dreamy comment about my life as a freelancer, I quietly counter with a balanced reality check. I feel vulnerable in sharing so honestly with all. But also . . . strong. My words are not weak, whining, or defiant. I listen, too, and we exchange ideas. We're just people talking. I learn more about others as they open up and talk back with me.

I came in solo. I stay sober.

When my body signals I'm done, I get my things to go.

A final colleague friend says goodbye: "Whatever you're doing, keep doing it because you look great."

This stops me for a second.

I've known this man for a while—we've spent time together at events and caught up over dinner. He's heard my health struggles and witnessed me in bedraggled state. Tonight, my eyes are clear. My soft smile is genuine. We've talked among others and occasionally shared a friendly touch.

I decide to trust that he sees *me* through the lost pounds and makeup.

"Thank you!" We warmly hug goodbye.

Yes. My power suit is knowing who I am. Then owning it.

Three weeks into this Final Forty Challenge, I lie awake. Hazy thoughts, not panic, keep me from sleep. The light around my eyes hovers a deep blue-gray. I try to focus on the ceiling, but something is floating over my head, blocking my view? I'm tired, and I don't know what I see. A cloud progressively hovers closer and closer to the artwork that hangs on the wall behind me; a masterpiece of #2 pencil and one of my most cherished possessions, it was drawn by a man who once loved me. From deep within, I hear a new voice boom:

"Move it. N*ow*." Petrified, I jump onto the bed, move my hands up the wall, feel where wire meets hook, and lift the heavy frame. I slide the piece to the floor and lay it on its side. I crawl back into bed. Blue fades to black. I sleep.

The next morning, moving from a place of intuition, I spend One Day with lovers past. I pick up a photograph of a vibrant red flower and a melodramatic memory of when He said, "This flower is you"; a stone statue of two faces pressed together called Devotion; sketchbooks, music lyrics, and photos. None trap lingering romantic feelings; I've kept them as sweet reminders of love once shared. But it's time to make space. I layer them into an empty makeup case from my theater days. I click the case shut. I place it on a high closet shelf. I feel lighter.

I log into an old online dating account. Messages flood in.

By that evening, I have a date planned with an artist we'll call Brush.

"Every single experience can be filtered through the view of a card," Tarot Sasha says when I bring her back on to *Love Bites*. "One of the joys of the deck is learning how to put your life on top of it." Every week since our show last October, I've pulled a card in the morning. The Knight of Swords—the same card she pulled for me then—has shown again several times. He's been my totem this Year, like having another Wonder Woman at my back, reminding me to be strong and sure. But it's time to let him go. In exploring vulnerability, I've learned that healthy relationships place trust in traversable walls, and the strongest person in the room needs no armored suit. If I'm to date again, I don't want to be the Knight I was with RoboWriter. But how will dating feel with armor off?

One Day with Brush, I test going without my Knight.

Brush, who has the most delightful smile.

We meet for lunch. We talk creative work, and our shared love of trees, dogs, and french fries. I mention I have a chronic illness only at the end. Brush doesn't poke. I don't expand. He asks me out again, kisses me goodbye, and follows up later by text. We meet the very next night for dinner, talk side-by-side for hours, and lay cards figuratively and literally; he rolls up a sleeve to reveal a tarot spread tattoo. I show him the Knight of Swords playing protector on my phone case. He pieces together, "Ah, so the card now warns you against building up emotional armor . . ." He doesn't flinch. He kisses me again. I go home smiling.

This Year, embracing my Knight got me through illness symptoms, romantic rejection, wells of loneliness, and absence of time with loved ones. Now stronger in my core, I'm ready to soften my surface.

"What you're describing is so part and parcel of the human condition," Tarot Sasha says. "Behaviors that once really protected us don't necessarily need to be with us five years into a situation. So whether it's a behavior, whether it's a tarot card, being able to let things go so that something new can come in is the healthiest thing you can do." Finding a new talisman can be as easy as deliberately picking one from the deck, she suggests, or regularly flipping and observing which most often comes to call.

I thank my Knight. I slip him back into the deck.

I shuffle three times. I cut once.

I flip the Ace of Cups. I see life bursting and overflowing—the scene tells me it's time to release withheld emotions. To not fear where they flow.

Ben and I talk about Brush on *Love Bites*. I share that, so far, I'm smitten. Ben asks if I let my mind wander to *happily ever after*. I tell him I don't; my illness often becomes too great a risk factor for men, and I can't let myself go there again. "It's been a problem in the past when

I've been less sick," I say into the mic. "Will there be a line for this guy? And if so, when is it?" I'm enjoying getting to know Brush. I want to keep my heart open. To date with no expectations.

And I do.

I observe that Brush is kind.

I discern that Brush is sweet and warmly communicative.

I sense that Brush really wants someone to love.

But then . . . I discover that Brush has some familiar doubts.

I Sherlock he's projecting baggage from his past on to our future.

I gather he has some deep emotional work to do for himself.

I decide I won't do the work this time.

I find my line.

I gently cut it.

But I'm okay this time.

Whether looking in a mirror or only inside myself.

Whether coupled or alone.

I do not need to be the Knight of Swords anymore.

I am human. A messy, calm, competent human.

I am enough, the way I am.

AUTONOMY AND AUTHENTICITY

(Physical Health, etc.)

About Time is one of my very favorite movies.

It's about an English family in which the men can jump time to specific experiences lived out in their pasts. We follow a charming father-and-son duo as the latter explores how best to practice this gift: If he learns from his growing pains, jumping back to fix mistakes, can he craft a perfectly happy life?

Writer and director Richard Curtis came upon the idea after a conversation with a friend challenged him to scrutinize the reality of his own happiness. His past romantic comedies (*Notting Hill, Bridget Jones's Diary, Love Actually,* etc.) had framed happiness as a romantic reward for a goal achieved. But when Curtis realized that his ideal day was not full of dramatic casino wins or Oscar nominations, but of dropping his kids at school, having lunch with a friend, and anticipating dinner with his family, he awakened to the awareness that true happiness often lies in our daily mundanity. He then crafted a time-traveling hero so to explore a choice: If you could relive each day to create your ideal life, with what would you fill it? "If that guy then decides that a perfect day would just be an ordinary day, then that might be a film worth watching," Curtis shares in an interview (not with me).[178]

We all have needs; material and psychological, met and unmet.

We all have struggles; great and small, lasting and fleeting.

The movie genre of our life depends on which view we choose to *savor.*

"We constantly strive for increased freedom and more opportunity to experience life in a self-directed manner," says Treadmill-Kasser of our need for *autonomy* and *authenticity.* "Rather than feeling pressured or burdened by our circumstances, we need to pursue activities that provide us with challenge, interest, and enjoyment." This Year, I've given in to even more acceptance that my health is not where I want it to be. But this Year also has provided me Challenges that help me forge on emotionally with greater confidence, despite my physical limitations. As my Final Forty days continue, I look to shape the movie of my life with the most joyful, present, self-directed hero I can craft.

One Weekend, I Challenge if I'm as tidy a woman as I think I am: I have to clean as I go and cannot leave anything dirty behind me. I wake and need to pee. But immediately pushed into the Challenge, I first must make the bed, pick up socks from the floor, bring water glasses into the kitchen, wash them (plus what's in the sink), and brush my teeth. Now I can pee! I walk back through a now-orderly apartment and properly rehang one coat before taking another to walk Mitra, then collapse into my chair to read Little Women, falling so engrossed I almost run late leaving for Connecticut; I frantically shower and am ready just as Mom arrives for me. (It's her fault I'm a book nerd anyway.) On my way out, I pause to appreciate how the tending sidestepped a tidying sprint at the end. At my mother's house on Mother's Day, I wash and wipe progressively as we cook. The house stands ready for guests, free of usual scramble. I particularly savor time with Nana as I sit before dessert, letting dirty dishes lie just for a few so that I can spend a little time immersed in her words.

One Day, I then do the opposite.

Some people (and studies) claim that clutter fosters focus: high-adrenaline environments force a mind to clear, a messy desk makes the brain think more creatively to connect dots, etc.[129] Constant tidying kept me continually in the present. If I let dirty things lie, can I savor the mess and make greater creative connections? I finish my coffee while blow-drying my hair, and both mug and machine stay where they are. Dishes progressively pile. Clothes mound on the floor and bed (which I don't make). My wallet explodes; I gather and drop the contents on the nearest shelf. I do not tidy as tea water boils, attentive to this without. I don't feel clear-headed as I write. My work is neither more creative nor abundant. I leave for yoga in an un–Zen-like state of panic—nothing is where I need it! I return home, exhausted, and can't crash in yoga-restored bliss to sip tea and continue my love/hate viewing of Anne with an E—tomorrow I'm abstaining from electricity, and so if I'm going to clean in corners that only see natural light, the time is now!

Cleaning the chaos takes over two hours.

I do not savor this One Day.

But the next?

I wake naturally to meet bright sunlight. It takes forty minutes to make coffee on the stovetop (gas range) because the beans aren't ground right for my Moka pot and I can't fix them with the electric grinder. I have to start again, twice I have time. Being without a weather app, I look out the windows at passing neighbors to assess how to dress. I can't see my clothes in the dark closet, but being more aware of touch nowadays, I better know how they *feel*. I sit with *Little Women* in my corner armchair, reading first by sunlight and then, as the afternoon sky dampens with gray, aided by long tapered candles and short tea lights. Dear Friend Rebecca comes over for dinner (the refrigerator being the one caveat), and we dreamily eat and talk in the candle glow. In bed by eleven, I blow out all light from my little cave and fall asleep with no white noise to shroud me from the world.

One of my favorite emotional exercises picked up from Hypnotherapist-Higgins is to put music on and dance like nobody's watching. Literally. And so, One Day, I wake and step on to my yoga mat. I have no expectations; I'm just changing my morning habit. I hit Play, the room fills with Carrie Newcomer's voice, and my body tells me where it wants to go. The tiny bones in my feet crunch as I rise and press. I wave and twist, muscles rippling and melting down rib cage and spine. My hips creak as I plant my feet wide and bow low. My body sighs *thank you* as soft music and orange morning light get me out of my head and into the *yes* of a body opening. With the fading notes, I reach up to the sky, then bow to the nothing and everything that brought me to this Day.

The next One Day, I'm at my desk, stressed. Stress threatens to overwhelm. It looms, closing my throat and making my heart beat like a drum. I think back to a *Love Bites* interview with Cynthia Cherish Malaran, coordinated during the No Hustle Challenge. As DJ Cherish the Luv, Cynthia believes "music heals." She would know; she survived both amnesia from a traumatic brain injury and aggressive breast cancer. "Music is a great way to take breaks," Cynthia said of minimizing stress to stay healthy.

CUE: Work rejection.

ROUTINE: ~~Brownie. Amazon. Spiral inside.~~ Dance it Out.

REWARD: Blood moves, the world shifts. I can handle this.

It took all of four minutes to "Shake It Off" with Taylor Swift.

One Day, Mitra and I try yet another new morning walking route. This time I bring my nose, eyes, and ears into alert, trying to deacclimate my brain from its adapted norm. *Whoa! It's spring in New York City!* The air fills with drooping jasmine and a chorus of chirping sparrows! A suited man walks by, and I almost faint in the overwhelming burst of his cologne. I find light in secreted nooks. I see mulberries on the ground; a surprise to my eyes, as the two mulberry trees on my street won't be lush with fruit for at least another month. We haven't walked this stretch of street since autumn leaves were dropping. Now the shade of fresh treetops cools the air. It fills with the high-pitched cries of baby birds. I wonder if I ever would have discovered just how much I need this solo, quiet, exploratory time with my dog were it not for this experiencing-my-experience journey? I lock in gratitude as we wind toward home.

I'm nearing the end of this Year.

My muscle for Challenging habit and observing change is strong.

I feel. I savor. I am present.

I move through One Day in silence. I'm thankful I've trained Mitra with hand gestures as well as words; as we move together from one room to another, I seek out her eyes and motion in a second language she knows well. We walk. I can't help but return a "hello" to a neighbor. A tiny toddler face with a giant smile makes a beeline for Mitra's wagging tail, with the proud grandfather I know well running after him. I use a few rich, purposeful words. Other than that, I listen.

In the quiet, I think to one of my spiritual teachers, Swami Satchidananda Saraswati. I found his Integral Yoga when sick again in my late twenties. Reading his perspectives on being "easeful, peaceful, and useful" through exploration of the true self, as well as the meditation and restorative yoga I've learned through his students, have significantly contributed to my physical and emotional health. In one of his recordings, Swamiji touches on how even the most mundane motions can become acts of devotion if we recognize the spark of divinity that lives inside all of us. "When you do everything for the sake and joy of just doing it, as a benefit for the whole world and not for your own personal benefit, you retain your joy," Swamiji says. "Don't think that you get joy by doing this—the joy is in you always. You must do something, because you can't simply sit there quietly doing nothing. Your actions allow you to retain the Supreme joy."[130]

I started this Year not knowing what to call my lost *it*.

Now I realize, I don't call *it* by name.

I see *it* when wind meets and rustles the leaves of trees, making all the world sway. It reflects from Mitra's eyes when they gaze up in that sloppy, unconditional love. I see *it* soaring in the grace of the hawk I spy while swinging in my hammock. I read *it* in the books that humans, like warriors, have wrested from the deepest caverns of their souls. I feel *it* when laughing with my siblings or sharing a good meal with my parents. It flies in the prayers of my grandparents. I hear it in the voice of someone who loves me, when they pull me from the brink back to the center. Carrie Newcomer sings, "If holy is a sphere that cannot be rendered, there is no middle place because all of it is centered." She does "not know its name," and neither do I.

But I find it everywhere now.

And I carry it inside too.

June 19, I leisurely drive from Connecticut to New York, chatting with Big Sis the entire time about nothing in particular. En route via subway to Brooklyn for *Love Bites*, I pause for a few words with the smiling men who sell me potato chips at the tunnel kiosk. I watch kids dig out the very last drops of ice cream from tubs the size of their faces. I observe strangers in random discussion, laughing like friends. I see couples lean against each other in casual comfort. I drop all the singles in my worn wallet into a hippie's faded violin case. I swoon over smushy-faced dogs on the sidewalk. I snoop the spines of hardcovers read around me at the coffee shop.

It's a perfect ordinary day of it everywhere.

Or as Richard Curtis might write it:

"If you look for it, I've got a sneaky feeling you'll find that *love* actually is all around." [131]

FULFILLED

PHYSICAL BODY: On our last *Love Bites* episode recorded during the Year, Ben asks: "Would you rather be completely free of your chronic illness from this point forward but never be able to find a committed romantic relationship ever, or continue on with your unpredictable debilitating health issues but find your lifelong romantic partner today?" Once again vulnerable with the On the

Air sign glowing, I can only whisper: "I would give up my illness. Yeah, I would give up being sick and be single forever." I'm afraid of where my illness has leveled. It hurts. But it's not my fault. I can't abstain from it. And I'm still pretty fucking okay with my life.

SOCIALIZATION: This Year, I learned to be present through solitude and not feel lonely while alone. But people bring me joy. So I have to Challenge myself to get out of my comfort zone. I have to go to more pastry parties, radio events, and coffee shops. I have to socialize and meet people. I tell Ben, "I'm pushing myself to do it."

SENSE OF SELF: I now know what things I love in my life, and I own that I love them. I love old books. I love smushy-faced dogs. I love yellow and antique rugs and Anne of Green Gables "I'm so damned in the moment, it's ridiculous. I feel like Unbreakable Kimmy Schmidt . . . inside my head," I joke to Ben about owning up to my nerdy side. He jabs that nothing would be left of me if I didn't. I can live with that conclusion.

***

Wednesday, June 21, 2017.
I wake happy.
Happy. Period.

I brush my teeth with homemade toothpaste. I notice sunlight speckling in through the window, smile too wide in response, and laugh while it dribbles from my mouth. Mitra and I take to the streets. I let her lead us on another unfamiliar route. I snuggle dogs I've never met before. I compliment a stranger's shirt, easeful in the exchange. We lazily wind our way home.

A few weeks ago, New York City unveiled a new composting program. Now, every Wednesday morning, I drop food scraps off to a tent set by the subway. I pull the bin from my freezer and add this morning's coffee grounds. I blend and press the almonds I've had soaking into milk, then add their sticky pulp to the bin too. Mitra and I head back out and drop the bag. I return to my desk. I work. I meet Dearie Darling Erin for lunch. We settle into a diner booth, and I pester her with questions about her expanding belly. (Auntie Jax!) Then we discuss this One Day's significance:

One Year ago, today. I was sick, single, broke, and wandering in a fog.

I am still sick, and my illness is worse.

I am still single, despite those many *noms de guerre.*

I am still broke, working as hard now to make ends meet as I did then. But…

I'm in pain, and I'm happy period.

I'm single, and I'm happy period.

I'm broke, and I'm happy period.

And when I'm freaking out about being sick, single, and broke, I have a bag of tools to help me tackle those justifiable, messy, human fears. I don't suppress them. I don't eat or drink them away. I don't soothe myself with a superficial purchase or hollow reward. One Year later, I know what I love, value, need, and want more than ever before. The smoke and mirrors, the rose-colored glasses, and the veils I didn't even realize I wore? Gone.

Ever so insightful, Erin reflects that these bits of personality were already a part of my puzzle; the puzzle was just put loosely together. The pieces needed adjustment, then a final click. Should I now go out and get a celebratory *something* to mark the very last day of this Year? A massage? A piece of jewelry? A museum visit?

I decide I don't need a celebration.

For my final Challenge, I go without reward.

June 21, 2017, is the reward.

Moving through My Day—the delightful unmundanity of brushing teeth, making milk, walking with Mitra, reading books, having lunch with a friend, doing work, and then stopping at the coffee shop on the way home to write while sipping iced tea—I'm rewarded over and over again. I reflect on the Challenges, the experiences, and the experience-of-the-experience I've given my best over these 365 days. I am present with every human. Every sensation. I enjoy this very moment.

(Typing that, I smile. Reading over this, a smile again.)

And the single-sick-broke trifecta?

I'm not disappointed they haven't shifted. I promise.

Because I trust I am standing on the precipice of something big.

I don't know what it is, again, this next turn in the path.

But isn't that what walking the path of change is about?

Savoring the discovery, the mess, the pain, the redemption?

The promise of what lies just beyond?

I trust that something is coming for me in love, health, or work.

I feel possibility moving in the periphery.

When it comes . . . when *they* come . . .

I will be ready.

I am ready.

I am.

Because of this Year.

AN EPILOGUE

On April 10, 1841, Thoreau recorded in his journal:

"How much virtue is there in simply seeing . . . The woman who sits in the house and *sees* is a match for a stirring captain. Those still piercing eyes, as faithfully exercised as their talent, will keep her even with Alexander or Shakespeare. They may go to Asia with parade, or to fairyland, but not beyond her ray. We are as much as we see . . ."

April 10, 2018, I sit in front of a broad picture window.

I see the open Pennsylvania sky, this midmorning striped top to bottom with white, gray, slate, and then pale-blue. Below it, I see the lake is rimmed with a light dusting of fresh snow. I see black eyed juncos and fox sparrows and tufted titmouse, hopping from one perch to the next. I see Narcissus and Ladybird; the pair of cardinals here I've named so for his habit of continually bashing into his reflection in Lil' Blue's side mirror while she ignores him, preening and pecking at the ground.

I'm in Cynthia Cherish Malaran's "Healing House" in the Pocono Mountains. My Year, Without pushed me to fulfill the promise I made to myself last winter: "to borrow a house in the woods so that my body has a place to restore during trying northern months." I'm here alone, writing the book *The Me, Without*.

Every day, for a little over three months now, I've awoken long before dawn. I slowly make coffee and spread seeds for birds I've

217

learned how to identify by quick glance. I feed Mitra and let her out to play in snow that hasn't stopped falling. Then I sit in front of this large window and write. When I need to fully ponder a thought, I let my gaze soften on the trees that sway in a crescent around us. I take in the sky as it shifts color by the minute. I absorb the woodland sounds: the peep of a woodpecker before he tears into suet, the specific flutter of a chickadee's flight; or my dog's sudden fury at the deer who dare to tread our land. When too sore to sit, I stretch my worn body in front of the woodstove I've kept blazing. I read my Thoreau *Early Spring* journal. I savor these purposeful, solitary days.

I am not lonely.

A few weeks into this new life, I stop and laugh.

I am the future self I saw in all those meditations.

It's here that I call Professor David DeSteno, Pilates Marcia Polas, Designer-Anthropologist Amber Case, and the many other voices in this story. Please forgive me for blending time lines, as I studied much of their work during the Year but only speak to them while organizing thoughts after. It's also here, while surrounded by mounds of deep-winter snow, that I reach Happy-Roko Belic at his California beach home. We share a meandering conversation; two artists still contemplating the intangible concepts of habit, healing, and happiness. I ask him: *If so many of us take action to be happier, why aren't we?* He asks back: Why don't more of us "fire roll into a positive happiness bliss spiral? I've never heard of a rehab place for somebody who is so blissed out they can't function."

Good point. None of his sources could answer that question.

We start at the hedonic treadmill: humans adapt to good things, and so whatever we think might make us happy (or happier) remains always just out of reach. Then there's dopamine; as we age, those happiness neurotransmitters naturally fire less often in our brain by around 10 percent per decade,[132] making it harder to feel pleasure without an (often damaging) quick fix. Then add Lyubomirsky's conclusion on changing up happiness habits; if we don't, the brain will level even to things like counting blessings. "I think it may simply be both edges of that sword of adaptation," Roko says.

He tells me of a discussion with P. Read Montague, a Virginia Tech neuroscientist who has pioneered understanding in how neurotransmission works in the brain, especially those altered by disease and injury. "He said your nervous system is essentially a 'difference engine'—it notices changes or what's different," Roko relays. "So if you walk into your living room one hundred times in one hundred days, you're not going to notice the books on the bookshelf and the pictures on the wall. But if there's suddenly a gorilla in the living room, you'll notice that immediately."[133]

We often notice a gorilla as the guy who cuts us off on the highway or the grocery store line that takes forever or the train we're on that the MTA takes out of commission. But if we notice those things because they're *different*, because they're *not our norm*? "What it means is that we're pretty goddamn well off most of the time," Roko chooses to conclude. Or as Carrie Fisher put it: "A problem derails your life and an inconvenience is not being able to get a nice seat on an un-derailed train."[134]

As I continue in the analysis and book-writing process, I can't shake Montague's "difference engine." Metaphorically speaking, I feel like my body notices a changed book in the room like someone else does the gorilla: a shift of light or loud sound sends me dizzy; I can't process words if music or television also plays; and I never would have enough daily energy or focus to write this large project if not entirely alone, in the woods. I use the phrase on others with similar illness conundrums, and—*yes!*—it's like our difference engines run continually on a higher gear. I haven't been able to diet, doctor, or mind-over-matter my way down yet. And I will never stop seeking greater health. But until those get sorted out, I wonder:

Can we better calibrate to notice *positive* differences?

Can we notice the human on the highway who only gently taps their horn to warn us against danger? The friendly grocery clerk? The fellows sharing a kind word while we're all delayed? Can we relay to loved ones the simply happy scene we saw exchanged on the street? The blissfully speedy subway?

I like to think so.

I like to think this Year tapped me into positive sensitivity.

Ripping off bandages, I first removed the panic architecture that welcomes nasty gorillas. Redirecting energy from outward physical stuff to inward emotional me, I explored intrinsic values and psychological needs. Better understanding them, I then started to fill my physical and emotional space with the things I know most make me happy.

I did not anticipate any of this would happen.

But happier habits kept building after June 21.

Now, I notice beauty everywhere.

I relish the treasure hunt for joyful stuff: at our next town-wide tag sale, I found pale yellow vintage drapes that now lushly hang against my golden-yellow accent wall. A neighbor left a heavy wooden desk with a leather top on the sidewalk; Bro' helped me transport and lightly restore it, I named her Louisa (May Alcott), and she's the most mysterious, sturdy, golden-brown beauty this writer could have asked for. On Louisa, a "favorite things" corner holds beloved plants I reroot and gift to friends. It holds acorns and dried leaves collected from three miraculous weeks of "going deep" in the Massachusetts woods with FW Lyndsey. It holds the tiny stump of Roomie Erika's and my last Christmas tree; a Christmas I spent laughing with the Riverside Writers and watching Mom joyfully dance around her festively decorated home. It holds a watercolor painting of a thistle shaped into a J; a gift from the artist from whom I bought some letters to spell the name of Dearie Darling Erin's beautiful new baby girl. It holds my golden Ganesh and Mother Mary. It holds a frame for the daily changing tarot talisman.

These help keep me happier as I work.

I look at food shopping like a game, taking cloth bags to bulk bins and welcoming delivery as if I've won a prize. Composting is a growing adventure. I successfully make deodorant and repeatedly fail at making cold cream. I build a badass costume with fabulous secondhand clothing. I simplify and strengthen my commitment to the natural world with *refuse* and *reduce*.

I spend even more hours curled in my corner chair. By the end of the Year in June, my library receipt showed I'd saved two hundred fifty dollars in lends since starting the No Shopping Challenge. The new Thoreau is one from a stack Mom and I found while rummaging a used bookstore on our way back to Newport, Rhode Island; I came home with Brontës and L. M. Montgomery too. I seek out other authors who believe in natural and magic realism: Frances Hodgson Burnett, Pam Muñoz Ryan, Richard Bach, and Eowyn Ivey.

These help me start believing in fairyland again too.

I flip tarot cards, marveling with Tarot Sasha how My Year, Without was full of active swords but now shifts to the creative support of rods. Hypnotherapist-Higgins takes me deep in private sessions; I continue to work on planning, accepting, releasing, and ebbing overwhelm.

I slow down on walks.

I slow down when considering a purchase.

I slow down when being gently honest in conversation.

I turn thirty-six in the company of real-life Wonder Women.

I savor and notice and see.

Months pass.

So many gentle *withs* and *additions* that are entirely another story.

Summer turns over into fall.

And I fall in love.

We met during the Year, at the pastry party I muscled down to in a yellow sweater when the No Television Challenge forbade a Sunday binge. I'd noticed then that he was cute. And that I liked his warm shyness. I wasn't ready to see more. I had more *without* to do. Then more taking in.

In September, I was ready. I saw him. My Mr. CPG.

His very real name is Daniel.

He is more than any set of words I could pen on paper.

Soon after, better-paying work started to come in.

Then the invitation to bring this book to your hands.

And now, here I sit, at a window.

Seeing stories of my past, present, and future.

Am I really here? Did this all happen?

I started this Year in a fog, not seeing the path.

Then I saw the path but did not know where it led.

My Year, Without forced me to pay attention to the journey.

I paid attention to the pain of wounds exposed and then the beautiful subtlety of smoothed scars. I learned to stop, sit, and contemplate the next steps I could take. I encountered some on the path who had, to my surprise, been on it with me always. I met others for the first time, whose paths now constantly intertwine with mine. I often thought I walked alone but then learned we rarely walk alone. And though, at the start, I contemplated overcoming a sick-single-broke trifecta, I now know my happiness doesn't rely on health, romance, or wealth. They are not the end of this path.

There is no end of this path.

There is only the path.

The point is to see and savor it.

YOUR YEAR, WITHOUT

Crafting My Year, Without pushed me to uncover, discover, and savor the long path. Throughout this project, and during cleanses and medical treatments in the past, I've spoken with others who struggle with long-term self-discipline and motivation, their lives are *fine*, and so best-laid plans for lasting change often fall flat. We discuss how maybe sticking through Challenge is clearer when the goal is normalcy?

I don't want someone to experience trauma before they start striving.

How can we shake things up without forced action?

I ask Professor David.

"A big life event helps you refocus and often makes you think about *'Well, what do I value? What should I be grateful for?'* I think for a lot of people, adversity is kind of the kick in the butt they need to make change. But if you practice mindfulness, you will be more compassionate, you will be more patient. If you practice gratitude, it will just make you behave in a way automatically."

I ask Happy-Home Rebecca.

"We can be paralyzed by having too much to do or too many choices. Look at something very manageable and go: *I can do five minutes; I can take the garbage out to the street.* If you just take these tiny action steps, then you build this little bit of momentum and that builds confidence: you're making a choice, your choice is successful, you're not afraid to make another choice. That is the hamster wheel of joy you end up on, right? Each action leads to another very doable action."

Hamster wheel of joy?

Much more fun than a hedonic treadmill!

If you're still reading this—hi!—maybe you're considering a Challenge for yourself? Excellent! I've thrown around a lot of words about what my journey was about. At its core though: I went without some stuff, and I observed what happened within. That's all. Following, I offer only insight and a few more words from the supersmart human crew to get you started on your journey. And there are full resource lists and more fun at jacquelineraposo.com.

But, first, I'm stealing Treadmill-Kasser's similar guidance disclaimer in *The High Price of Materialism*; take this as my first wholehearted cheerlead in your head:

"What will be most exciting and growth-producing for you cannot be mass produced and sold; you must find it within yourself."[135]

FIND YOUR WITHOUT

Throughout the Year, friends and online friends would suggest Challenges I should attempt. These often came after I (quickly) told them where I was on my path and they (at length) told me of trials met on theirs. More often than not, our struggles didn't overlap; they knew what habits they had to face, but I couldn't do that work for them. And so I gently reflected back, "That's your *without*."

Chances are you already have an idea of your *without* too. If your gut tells you something, go with it; "That's a good one to listen to," as CEO Sarah says. If you feel both scared and relieved at the idea of something being out of your life for a while, chances are it's the right thing to step off with.

If you have no idea where to start, then observe a few days of your life:

What actions do you regret not long after you've finished them?

What do you wish you had more time to do?

What time-sucker stopped you from getting to do that?

Ponder not doing that thing for a week or a month:

Do you notice a reaction in your body—how does it *feel*?

Consider taking that thing out.

You can always pick something new and start over.

SET IT UP AND SHAKE IT OFF

It's just a week, a month, or a year. You can do this. You deserve this.

SET YOURSELF UP FOR SUCCESS: If you are easily tempted with stuff in sight, purge your space of that stuff. If you do best with a little peer pressure, join a group or partner up with a Challenge buddy. If home life and regularity make it too hard to face change, then go somewhere else.

TAKE IT OUT: Pick a start date and length of time that make sense for you. I felt the first significant wave of change after ten days, then a deeper one around thirty-five or forty. Sixty and ninety days really made a difference. If easily intimidated, start simple: *I'll go without this for a week.* You can always extend while on the ride. Give yourself time to think through and prepare for Challenges, but not so much time that you'll never feel ready.

Use procrastination to your benefit. Start when you say you will.
Fail if you have to on Day One. But start.

EXPLORE YOUR CURIOSITIES

Autonomous change might be easy for you.
(If it is, message and tell me how, please.)
I find it helps to have teachers light the path.

Treadmill-Kasser says, "Indeed, research suggests that being
confronted with concrete information about the consequences and
implications of their values can lead people to change both their
values and the behaviors relevant to them."[136]

Teachers can be therapists, hypnotherapists, and psychiatrists.
Teachers can be books of faith and the religiously ordained.
Teachers can be tarot cards, numerologists, and astrologists.
Lists of my Teachers are updated on jacquelineraposo.com.
But this is Your Without. Don't be afraid to make yours.

FIND YOUR TEACHERS IN MUSIC: Make a Challenge playlist
of songs embodying emotions or values you seek, and queue
them up for a boost. Need inspiration? Type *song* and your habit
word into a search engine to get started. As DJ Cherish the Luv
professes, "Music heals." Crank it up, dance it out.

FIND YOUR TEACHERS IN MOVIES: Explore documentaries,
rom-coms, comedies, superhero action flicks—whichever help
you explore the habit or emotion you're navigating. Don't forget
to change it up: make an active plan to explore a theater or a
kind of film not in your routine.

FIND YOUR TEACHERS IN RESEARCH: Supersmart
researchers, dissectors, and anthropologists explain and expand

our understanding of humankind. Reading their studies sometimes takes patience, especially in the beginning. But as neurons fire and wire, the comprehension muscles work faster. It becomes a fascinating rabbit hole. There's plenty of room next to me in it.

FIND YOUR TEACHERS IN LITERATURE: I love Thriftbooks. com and Indiebound.org for used books I expect to scribble in. The public library is an excellent source for when you don't plan to put pen on pages or need a push to read before due dates. If you love something, review it on purchasing or sharing platforms (that helps authors). Share it or reach out to the person who wrote it via social media. Be an active part of the book nerd community. Toss a stone, watch for ripples, and be thankful for ripples that come your way.

EXPRESS YOURSELF

Daniel Gilbert's *experience* versus *awareness* thing stuck with me through my *entire* Year: "One gives us the sense of being engaged, whereas the other gives us the sense of being cognizant of that engagement," he says. "One denotes reflection, while the other denotes the thing being reflected."

This Year changed stuff because I recorded and reflected.

"We should draw pictures and journal—nobody journals anymore!" bemoans Anthropologist-Amber. "Get a special notebook. Keep a diary. Have some reflection time. At the end of every week, write down what you thought. Draw badly, sing badly, make music badly!"

Record Your Challenge. The medium doesn't matter.

I journaled in typed notes and on a blog. I scratched in Moleskins. I recorded thoughts in my phone via Siri.

I dissected with Ben on *Love Bites*.

I voice messaged FW Lyndsey. I texted SW Rose.

I even attempted to paint and color a little.

This provides documentation for comparison and reflection. It helps trigger greater awareness of the experience. It helps to focus the journey. Otherwise, it's easy to forget the path behind you, as well as not know what you hope to see ahead.

DO IT FOR YOU

One very dark day this Year, I worried: *Will this be worth it?*

Would the single-sick-broke trifecta shift? If there wasn't better health, big romance, a steady paycheck, or (after this was signed with my agent) a book deal by the end, would there be a purpose to my suffering?

It makes sense to want assurance that a reward is in sight. In this presentational world, we're primed to want our journey to "go viral." As Be-Zero Andrea said in regard to a zero waste lifestyle, "We want there to be an endgame; we want there to be a pat on the back and a certificate at the end. I tell people—there isn't. So don't expect it."

I had to quiet the dark-day demons and do My Year, Without for me. If I hadn't genuinely focused on each Challenge, none of this would have worked. It would have been an entire waste of time. Do this for you.

EMBRACE THE CHANGE

I still contend that life is hard.

Almost everyone has something another person wants. We can then factor in excess versus need, entitlement versus humility, and privilege versus marginalization. As Activist-King rallied at the March for Change, "Us hurting together brings us closer together, to fight for something better." As Carrie Fisher put it, "Sometimes life actually gives to you by taking away." As Anthropologist-Amber encouraged, "Allow yourself to hate yourself and to start to like yourself again." As my coffee shop chalkboard sign spelled out, "If it doesn't challenge you, it won't change you."

Yes, suffering can be a productive teacher.

But please stay attentive to the good during the bad.

At the end of *About Time*, our hero stops traveling back entirely. "I just try to live every day as if I've deliberately come back to this one day to enjoy it as if it was the full final day of my extraordinary ordinary life," he says. [137]

Each day starts and ends with whatever we choose to lock in.

When there's some good in Your Days Without, see and savor it.

DO IT AGAIN!

Happy-Home Rebecca observes, "Everyone's like, *Oh, you're a success overnight!* No, you're a success because of ten years of tiny little steps."

I still take tiny little steps on my happiness hamster wheel every day.

Because happiness is not a gift.

It's not something you win.

It's not easier to hold on to when you get the guy or the job; even wonderful things present new challenges and require unique tools. When something new comes in—good or bad—the scales shift. If we "don't have time" to *do* happy things or try new tactics, we revert to that baseline.

We have to put in the time.

We have to do the work.

"It's worth trying. It's worth the effort, the annoyance, the tediousness," Happy-Roko promises. Producing *Happy* encouraged him to move cities, focus on his relationships, and continue community-fostering film. This Year continues to encourage me more toward a life of intrinsic values. We tease ourselves about sounding "Pollyanna-ish." As I write this book, I sometimes roll my eyes at how Anne Shirley I sound too. But I agree with Roko: "It's worth getting into a world of fluffy, new agey words. It's worth tolerating some discomfort. Because the rewards are so much greater than the small negatives."

If one Challenge has served you well, put that card back in the deck.

Pick another.

Keep choosing teachers, stories, and scenes.

Observe. Experience your experience.

Change something. Savor something.

Learn something new about yourself and the world around you.

Be kind to yourself and others.

Be better tomorrow than you are today.

We only get one life. One habitable place.

Let's live within it.

ACKNOWLEDGMENTS

"So many people have helped me to come to this night. Some of you are here. Some are far away. Some are even in heaven. All of us have special ones who have loved us into being. Would you just take, along with me, ten seconds to think of the people who have helped you become who you are? Those who have cared about you, and wanted what was best for you in life? Ten seconds of silence. I'll watch the time..."

—Fred Rogers, accepting his Lifetime Achievement Emmy, 1997

If I've used your name in these pages, thank you for loving me—and this book into being. There are good people whose names are not on these pages because, as I said in my Invitation, "This is a book, and books require direction." Please trust your name is thought of during many ten-second pauses. I love you.

Dear Friend Rebecca Carlisle encouraged my writing a book long before My Year of Abstinence began. Her taking action catalyzed *The Me, Without*. Everyone should be so lucky to have a such a Dear Friend. Thank you, Rebecca, for being mine.

Thank you to my agent Stacey Glick at Dystel, Goderich &

Bourret LLC, for encouraging me forward. Thank you to my signing acquisitions editor Nora Rawn, for taking a chance and digging my quirk. Thank you to my Dover/Ixia Press editor Fiona Hallowell for supporting and patiently guiding me. Thank you to copy editor Sally Fay and editor Stephanie Castillo Samoy for tightly editing these pages and letting me learn from the process. To the collective Dover/ Ixia Press team: I am my best self when calmly inspired. Thank you for calmly inspiring me throughout this very big "first."

I wrote this book in the quiet isolation I've envisioned in every "future self" meditation because of Cynthia Cherish Malaran's generosity. Cynthia, thank you. I treasure that dream. Thank you to Roomie Erika Villalba, for making New York a special work-home, too. I also regularly write in the safe havens of the Wilton, Connecticut Public Library and the New York Public Library. Thank you, to those who support such spaces. And thank you, librarians everywhere.

A team of talented readers and writers looked at pages and shared insight. Paul Caiola, Max Falkowitz, Emma Cosgrove, Ben Rosenblatt, Lyndsey Ellis, and Rose Sabo are not only incredible talents in this, but also treasured friends. Thank you. Special thanks to SW Rose for reading every page of every draft. Your constant presence while I typed in the woods, *alone*, made all the difference. Thank you, also, to Riverside Writers Paul Caiola, Erika Villalba, Janet Matlock, and Meg Boyle, for your book proposal help and all the soul fluffing during this adventure. Your creative badassery inspires me.

Thank you, Carrie Fisher, Debbie Reynolds, Dr. John T. Cacioppo, Aunt Penny D'Ambrosio, and Professor Bob McDonald, who all passed away during this project. I often pause and think of you. (Bob, we'll keep the monologue going, buddy.)

My emotional health and self-identity in regard to living with illness fluctuate with time and shifting physical ability/inability.

My relationships ebb and flow with those, too. Requiring help is humbling. I've had many teachers guide me through this. They help me help others. (Stones and ripples, right?) Thank you especially to the teachers at Integral Yoga Institute and Sri Swami Satchidananda. Thank you to my constant heart-calmer, Daniel Neiden. Thank you to my soul-surging hypnotherapist, Iris Higgins. Thank you to my beloved godfather, Father Diogo Fernandes. Thank you to my soulmate and spirit guide, FW Lyndsey Ellis. Thank you to Hillary Clinton, and all who lift up, move forward, walk on, and go #MarchingWithMe.

I was entirely unprepared for how intellectually and emotionally rewarding writing this book would be. I was also entirely unprepared for the toll it would take on my body. Only because of these final people was I physically, emotionally, and intellectually able to write it.

Ben Rosenblatt—Thank you.

Daniel Skurnick—Thank you.

Rose Sabo and Rex King—Thank you.

Lyndsey Ellis and Christian Donaldson—Thank you.

My father, Dan Raposo, and Regina Zavaski—Thank you.

My mother, Doris D'Ambrosio—Thank you.

My grandparents, Pat and Hansine D'Ambrosio—Thank you.

My siblings, Jessica, Dan and Lizzie, and Maggie—Thank you.

And Mitra (who can't read this because she's a dog)—Thank you.

Thank you for being my family.

Thank you for being centering points, anchors, lifelines, and arrows.

Thank you for making my world full of joy and happiness.

Thank you for so much more than just this Year.

The word *love* is inefficient. But I love you.

Thank you for loving me into being.

I can go without everything but you.

NOTES

1   International Lyme and Associated Diseases Society, "Quick Facts," "40% OF LYME PATIENTS END UP WITH LONG TERM HEALTH PROBLEMS. The average patient sees 5 doctors over nearly 2 years before being diagnosed," http://www.ilads.org/lyme/lyme-quickfacts.php

2   International Lyme and Associated Diseases Society, "Quick Facts," "THERE ARE NO TESTS AVAILABLE TO PROVE THAT THE ORGANISM IS ERADICATED OR THAT THE PATIENT IS CURED," http://www.ilads.org/lyme/lyme-quickfacts.php

3   For more, consider: Cecilie Schou Andreassen, Ståle Pallesen, Mark D. Griffiths, "The relationship between addictive use of social media, narcissism, and self-esteem: Findings from a large national survey," *Addictive Behaviors*, Issue 64, March 2016, DOI: 10.1016/j. addbeh.2016.03.006; Keith Wilcox, Andrew T. Stephen, "Are Close Friends the Enemy? Online Social Networks, Self-Esteem and Self-Control," *Journal of Consumer Research*, Volume 40, Issue 1, 1 June 2013, pp 90–103, https://doi.org/10.1086/668794, Published: 27 November 2012.

4   https://twitter.com/thisisjendull/status/743371778961260544

5   Adeel Hassan, "Donald Trump, Orlando, Anton Yelchin: Your Tuesday Briefing," *The New York Times*, Jun 21, 2016, https://www.nytimes.com/2016/06/21/nytnow/your-tuesday-briefing-donald-trump-orlando-anton-yelchin.html

6   "Social Media Fact Sheet," Jan 12, 2017, Pew Research Center, http://www.pewinternet.org/fact-sheet/social-media/

7   Andrew Perrin, "One-fifth of Americans report going online 'almost constantly,'" Pew Research Center, Dec 8, 2015, http://www.pewresearch.org/fact-tank/2015/12/08/one-fifth-of-americans-report-going-online-almost-constantly/

8   Clifford Nass, "Is Facebook Stunting Your Child's Growth?" Pacific Standard, Apr 23, 2012

9   Sherry Turkle, *Reclaiming Conversation: The Power of Talk in a Digital Age*, Penguin Press, Oct 2015, Intro

10 Kristin Newman, *What I Was Doing While You Were Breeding*, Three Rivers Press, 2014

11 Amber Case, *Calm Technology*, O'Reilly Media, 2016, Ch. 2, "Principles of Calm Technology"

12 Kyle Stock, Lance Lambert, Dave Ingold, "Smartphones Are Killing Americans, But Nobody's Counting," Bloomberg, Oct 17, 2017

238   Notes

13   Sherry Turkle, *Reclaiming Conversation: The Power of Talk in a Digital Age*, Penguin Press, Oct 2015, p 38

14   Terra Barnes, Yasuo Kubota, Dan Hu, Dezhe Z Jin, Ann M Graybiel, "Activity of striatal neurons reflects dynamic encoding and recoding of procedural memories," *Nature*, 2005, 437. 1158-61. 10.1038/nature04053

15   "MIT researcher sheds light on why habits are hard to make and break," MIT *News*, Oct. 20, 1999

16   Charles Duhigg, *The Power of Habit*, Random House, 2012, Ch 1

17   Ed Diener, Jeff Horowitz, Robert A. Emmons, "Happiness of the Very Wealthy," R.A. Social Indicators Research, 1985, 16: 263. https://doi.org/10.1007/BF00415126

18   Tim Kasser, *The High Price of Materialism*, MIT Press, 2002

19   Tim Kasser, *The High Price of Materialism*, MIT Press, 2002, Ch. 2

20   Will S. Hylton, "The Unbreakable Laura Hillenbrand," *The New York Times Magazine*, Dec 18, 2014

21   Esmé Weijun Wang, "When Delivery Is Not a Luxury," *Eater*, Sept 27, 2016

22   "Sugar Industry and Coronary Heart Disease Research," *JAMA Network*, http://jamanetwork.com/journals/jamainternalmedicine/article-abstract/2548255

23   Anahad O'Connor, "How the Sugar Industry Shifted Blame to Fat," *New York Times*, Sept 12, 2016, https://www.nytimes.com/2016/09/13/well/eat/how-the-sugar-industry-shifted-blame-to-fat.html?_r=1

24   Jacqueline Raposo, "Don't Call Me Pretty, I'm Just Sick and Skinny," *Bust*, April 2016

25   For more on this, read Allie Cashel's *Suffering the Silence: Chronic Lyme Disease in an Age of Denial*, North Atlantic Books, 2015.

26   Riva P, Sacchi S, Montali L, Frigerio A, "Gender effects in pain detection: speed and accuracy in decoding female and male pain expressions," *Eur J Pain* 2011 Oct;15(9):985.e1-985.e11, doi: 10.1016/j.ejpain.2011.02.006, Epub 2011 Mar 23.

27   Judy Foreman, "Why Women are Living in the Discomfort Zone," *The Wall Street Journal*, Jan 31, 2014

28   David R. Williams, Harold W. Neighbors, James S. Jackson, "Racial/Ethnic Discrimination and Health: Findings From Community Studies," *American Journal of Public Health* 93, no. 2 (February 1, 2003): pp 200–208.

29   Penner LA, Blair IV, Albrecht TL, Dovidio JF, "Reducing Racial Health Care Disparities: A Social Psychological Analysis," *Policy Insights From the Behavioral and Brain Sciences*, 2014;1(1):204–212, doi: 10.1177/2372732214548430.

30   Izmirly PM, Wan I, Sahl S, Buyon JP, Belmont HM, Salmon JE, Askanase A, Bathon JM, Geraldino-Pardilla L, Ali Y, Ginzler EM, Putterman C, Gordon C, Helmick CG, and Parton H, "The Incidence and Prevalence of Systemic Lupus Erythematosus in New York County (Manhattan), New York: The Manhattan Lupus Surveillance Program," *Arthritis & Rheumatology*, 2017;69: 2006–2017, doi: 10.1002/art.40192

31   American Addiction Centers, http://americanaddictioncenters.org/withdrawal-timelines-treatments/

32   Maya Rhodan and David Johnson, "Here Are 7 Electoral College Predictions for Tuesday," *Time*, Nov 8, 2016, http://time.com/4561625/electoral-college-predictions/

33   "The Empire State Building has transformed into a giant, glowing election tracker tonight," *Washington Post*, Nov 8, 2016, https://www.washingtonpost.com/politics/2016/live-updates/general-election/real-time-updates-on-the-2016-election-voting-and-race-results/the-empire-state-building-has-transformed-into-a-giant-glowing-election-tracker-tonight/?utm_term=.601837ee09ae

34   All data throughout taken from Election 2016, *Washington Post*, Nov 8–9 2016, https://www.washingtonpost.com/politics/2016/live-updates/general-election/real-time-updates-on-the-2016-election voting and race-results/?utm_term= 4d2477b2d91a

35   *Washington Post*, Nov 8, 2016, https://www.washingtonpost.com/politics/2016/live-updates/general-election/real-time updates-on-the-2016-election-voting-and-race-results/electoral-vote-counter-who-has-the-lead/?utm_term= c120442879ac

36   Colby Itkowitz, *Washington Post*, "AP: Trump elected president," Nov 9, 2016, https://www.washingtonpost.com/politics/2016/live-updates/general-election/real-time-updates-on-the-2016-election-voting-and-race-results/ap-trump-elected-president/?utm_term=.81121662bd50

37   Bocarsly MF, Hoebel BG, Paredes D, von Loga I, Murray CM, Wang M, Arolfo MP, Yao L, Diamond I, Avena NM, "GS 455534 selectively suppresses binge eating of palatable food and attenuates dopamine release in the accumbens of sugar-bingeing rats," *Behav Pharmacol* 2014;25(2): 147–157, https://dl.dropboxusercontent.com/u/32738245/67Bocarsly14.pdf

38   Estimated from 2 servings of Cape Cod 40% Reduced Fat Potato Chips . . . my favorite; https://www.capecodchips.com/product/40 reduced-fat-original/

39   Iulia Bainbridge, "Why I Stopped Drinking on Dates," *Manrepeller*, 2016, http://www.manrepeller.com/2016/10/drinking-on-dates-alcohol.html

40   Daniel Gilbert, *Stumbling on Happiness*, First Vintage Books, 2005, Ch 3, p 66

41   Daniel Gilbert, *Stumbling on Happiness*, First Vintage Books, 2005, Ch 7, p 151

42   Anonymous, *True Politeness, A Hand-Book of Etiquette For Ladies*, Leavitt & Allen, 1847

43   From Charles Varle, *Moral Encyclopaedia*, 1830: "18 Rules of Behavior for Young Ladies in 1831," NPR History Department, https://www.npr.org/sections/npr-history-dept/2015/11/20/456224571/18-rules-of-behavior-for-young-ladies-in-1831

44   Keri Hanson, "The History of Macy's: From Humble Beginnings to Stunning Success," VisitMacys.com, https://www.visitmacysusa.com/article/history-macys-humble-beginnings-stunning-success

45   Walter R. Houghton, *American Etiquette and Rules of Politeness*, Standard Pub. Co., 1883

46   Lindy Woodhead, *Shopping, Seduction, and Mr. Selfridge*, Profile Books, 2007

47   Keri Hanson, "The History of Macy's: From Humble Beginnings to Stunning Success," VisitMacys.com, https://www.visitmacysusa.com/article/history-macys-humble-beginnings-stunning-success

48   Jonathan Glancey, "A History of the Department Store," BBC *Culture*, Mar 26, 2015

49   Helen Fielding, *Bridget Jones's Diary*, Viking, 1998

50   "Ringing in the Holidays: Hershey's Kisses Chocolates," HersheyArchives.org, http://blog
.hersheyarchives.org/tag/tv-commercial/

51   "Why Are We Not Happier During Christmas?" *The New York Times*, Dec 23, 2012, https://www
.nytimes.com/roomfordebate/2012/12/23/why-arent-people-happier-during-the-holidays/the-
holidays-offer-mixed-blessings

52   Stephanie Cacioppo, John P. Capitanio, John T. Cacioppo, "Toward a Neurology of Loneliness,"
Psychological Bulletin, Nov 2014, Vol 140(6), 1464–1504

53   John T. Cacioppo et al., "Lonely traits and concomitant physiological processes: the MacArthur
social neuroscience studies," *International Journal of Psychophysiology*, 2000;35:143–154

54   John T. Cacioppo et al., "Lonely traits and concomitant physiological processes: the MacArthur
social neuroscience studies," *International Journal of Psychophysiology*, 2000;35:143–154

55   Brinkhues et al., "Socially isolated individuals are more prone to have newly diagnosed and
prevalent type 2 diabetes mellitus - the Maastricht study," BMC *Public Health*, 2017;17:955, doi
10.1186/s12889-017-4948-6

56   Stephanie Cacioppo, John P. Capitanio, John T. Cacioppo, "Toward a Neurology of Loneliness,"
Psychological Bulletin, Nov 2014, Vol 140(6), 1464–1504

57   John T. Cacioppo et al., "Lonely traits and concomitant physiological processes: the MacArthur
social neuroscience studies," *International Journal of Psychophysiology*, 2000;35:143–154

58   Taken from attendance at Charles Dickens and The Spirit of Christmas, The Morgan Library &
Museum, New York City, http://www.themorgan.org/exhibitions/charles-dickens-and-the-spirit-
of-christmas

59   Thomas Hood, "A Christmas Carol in Prose," Hood's Magazine and Comic Miscellany: Volume
1, January 1, 1844, H. Hurst

60   Lisa Feldman Barrett, "The Secret History of Emotions," *The Chronicle Review*, Mar 5, 2017

61   Lisa Feldman Barrett, "The Secret History of Emotions," *The Chronicle Review*, Mar 5, 2017

62   Lisa Feldman Barrett, James Gross, Tamlin Conner Christensen, Michael Benvenuto, "Knowing
what you're feeling and knowing what to do about it: Mapping the relation between emotion
differentiation and emotion regulation," *Psychology Press*, 2001;15 (6):713–724

63   "The Unsinkable Debbie Reynolds Looks Back on Life, Love, and a Boozy Busby Berkeley,"
NPR Weekend Edition, Mar 27, 2013

64   Carrie Fisher, *Wishful Drinking*, Simon & Shuster, 2008

65   Emilie M. Townes, A *Troubling in My Soul: Womanist Perspectives on Evil and Suffering*, Orbis Books, 1993

66   Erica Chenoweth and Jeremy Pressman, "This is what we learned by counting the women's
marches," *The Washington Post*, Feb 7, 2017

67   Samantha Michaels, "The Americans With Disabilities Act is Turning 25. Watch the Dramatic
Protest that Made It Happen," *Mother Jones*, July 25, 2015

68   Sara Barton, "Geeking Out About #MarchingWithMe," *Geeks Out*, Feb 14, 2017

69   Angela Davis, "To the 3 Women Who Rallied For My Rare Disease at the Women's March," *The Mighty*, February 7, 2017

70   Emile M. Townes, "Living in the New Jerusalem: The Rhetoric and Movement of Liberation in the House of Evil," A *Troubling in My Soul: Womanist Perspectives on Evil and Suffering*, Orbis Books, 1993

71   Rev. Dr. Kathryn N. Dwyer, "Why Is There Suffering?" Rock Spring Congregationalist United Church of Christ, Mar 25, 2018, http://www.rockspringucc.org/media/why-is-there-suffering

72   Mark King at the March For Our Lives, Video, https://youtu.be/4GSFjXd_Ibs

73   Susan Dominus, "When the Revolution Came for Amy Cuddy," *The New York Times*, Oct 18, 2017

74   Dana R. Carney, Amy J.C. Cuddy, Andy J. Yap, "Power Posing: Brief Nonverbal Displays Affect Neuroendocrine Levels and Risk Tolerance," *Psychological Science*, Vol 21, Issue 10, pp 1363–1368, Sept 20, 2010

75   Joseph P. Simmons, Leif D. Nelson, Uri Simonsohn, "False-Positive Psychology: Undisclosed Flexibility in Data Collection and Analysis Allows Presenting Anything as Significant," *Psychological Science*, Vol 22, Issue 11, pp 1359–1366, Oct 17, 2011

76   Eva Ranehill, Anna Dreber, Magnus Johannesson, Susanne Leiberg, Sunhae Sul, Roberto A. Weber, "Assessing the Robustness of Power Posing: No Effect on Hormones and Risk Tolerance in a Large Sample of Men and Women," *Psychological Science*, Vol 26, Issue 5, pp 653–656, Mar 25, 2015

77   David DeSteno, "A Feeling of Control: How America Can Finally Learn to Deal with Its Impulses," *Pacific Standard*, Sept 15, 2014

78   Annie Leonard, The Story of Stuff video, https://storyofstuff.org/movies/story-of-stuff/

79   http://zwia.org/standards/zw-definition/

80   Josh Sandbulte, "Why the Post Office Gives Amazon Special Delivery," *The Wall Street Journal*, July 13, 2017

81   Clare Miflin, Juliette Spertus, Benjamin Miller, Christine Grace, "Zero Waste Design Guidelines: Design Strategies and Case Studies for a Zero Waste City," The Center for Architecture, 2017

82   Compared between Fresh Direct's Family Sized Tub of Raw Almonds and Westerly Market's raw almonds in bulk, https://www.freshdirect.com/pdp.jsp?productId=gro_fd_tb_rawalm&catId=gro_ntsd_almnd and http://www.westerlynaturalmarket.com/shop/product_view.asp?id=1046804&StoreID=QWCSN3N89ASR2JS000AKHMCCQAB04FN2&private_product=1

83   Victor Lebow, "Price Competition in 1955," *Journal of Retailing*, Spring 1955

84   Luke Whelan, "4 Big Recycling Myths Tossed Out," *Mother Jones*, Jul 13, 2015

85   Roland Geyer, Jenna R. Jambeck, Kara Lavender Law, "Production, use, and fate of all plastics ever made," *Science Advances*, July 19, 2017, E1700782

86 Advancing Sustainable Materials Management: 2014 Fact Sheet, Environmental Protection Agency, https://www.epa.gov/sites/production/files/2016-11/documents/2014_smmfactsheet_508.pdf

87 The State of Connecticut Department of Energy and Environmental Protection, Apr 2018, www.ct.gov

88 Luke Whelan, "4 Big Recycling Myths Tossed Out," *Mother Jones*, Jul 13, 2015

89 Arlington, VA, Department of Environmental Services Quarterly Review, January 2018 for calendar year 2016

90 Provided by MOM'S Organic Market

91 Clean Water Action, "The Problem of Marine Plastic Pollution," https://www.cleanwater.org/problem-marine-plastic-pollution. Sourced from: D.W. Laist, "Impacts of marine debris: entanglement of marine life in marine debris including a comprehensive list of species with entanglement and ingestion records," in Coe JM, Rogers DB (eds), *Marine Debris: Sources, Impacts, and Solutions*, Springer-Verlag, New York, 1997, pp 99–139

92 Joseph H. Guth, "Law for the Ecological Age," *Vermont Journal of Environmental Law*, Volume 9, 2007–2008

93 Advancing Sustainable Materials Management: 2014 Fact Sheet, United States Environmental Protection Agency Office of Land and Emergency Management (5306P), Nov 2016. Nondurable waste includes clothing, footwear, drapery, etc. Overall textiles rates that include leather and rubber make the numbers even higher. Number calculated = Total weight = 11.95 million tons = 23,900,000,000 pounds / 2014 population of US at 318.6 million = 75.02 lb per person

94 Elizabeth Cline, "Where Does Discarded Clothing Go?" *The Atlantic*, July 18, 2004

95 Angel Chang, "The life cycle of a t-shirt," TED-Ed

96 Bangladesh Factsheet, Clean Clothes Campaign, Feb 2015, https://cleanclothes.org/resources/publications/factsheets/bangladesh-factsheet-2-2015.pdf/view

97 Andrea Newell, "Soon Your Clothes Could Be as Recyclable as Glass or Paper. Really," Story of Stuff Project, https://storyofstuff.org/blog/soon-your-clothes-could-be-as-recyclable-as-glass-or-paper-really/

98 Ashley Westerman, 4 Years After Rana Plaza Tragedy, What's Changed For Bangladeshi Garment Workers?, NPR, Apr 30, 2017

99 "According to Greenpeace, global clothing production doubled from 2000 to 2014. The average person buys 60 percent more items of clothing every year and keeps them for about half as long as 15 years ago," Rick LeBlanc, "Textile Recycling Facts and Figures," *The Balance*, Dec 29, 2017

100 Advancing Sustainable Materials Management: 2014 Fact Sheet, United States Environmental Protection Agency Office of Land and Emergency Management (5306P), Nov 2016

101 Elizabeth Cline, "Where Does Discarded Clothing Go?" *The Atlantic*, July 18, 2004

102 Angel Chang, "The life cycle of a t-shirt," TED-Ed

103   Andrea Newell, "Never Look at Clothes the Same Way Again," Story of Stuff Project, https://storyofstuff.org/blog/never-look-at-clothes-the-same-way-again/

104   Megan Garber, "Turns Out, Rory Gilmore is Not a Good Journalist," *The Atlantic*, Nov 28, 2016

105   Stacy Lu, "Too Much Caffeine?" *American Psychological Association*, Nov 2015, p 20, http://www.apa.org/gradpsych/2015/11/coffee.aspx

106   Lenore Arab, Faraz Khan, Helen Lam, "Epidemiologic Evidence of a Relationship between Tea, Coffee, or Caffeine Consumption and Cognitive Decline," *Adv Nutr* Jan 4, 2013 (1):115–122, doi: 10.3945/an.112.002717

107   Caffeine content for coffee, tea, soda, and more, The Mayo Clinic, as of Mar 2018, https://www.mayoclinic.org/healthy-lifestyle/nutrition-and-healthy-eating/in-depth/caffeine/art-20049372

108   Food and chemical toxicology: an international journal published for the British Industrial Biological Research Association, ISSN: 1873-6351, Vol: 109, Issue: Pt 1, pp 585–648

109   Lisa Drayer, "The caffeine 'detox': How and why to cut back on your daily fix," CNN, Oct 20, 2017

110   Jonah Lehrer, "Don't! The secret of self-control," *The New Yorker*, May 18, 2009

111   Tanya R. Schlam, et al., "Preschoolers' Delay of Gratification Predicts their Body Mass 30 Years Later," *The Journal of Pediatrics*, 2013, Volume 162, Issue 1, pp 90–93

112   Jonah Lehrer, "Don't! The secret of self-control," *The New Yorker*, May 18, 2009

113   David DeSteno, "A Feeling of Control: How America Can Finally Learn to Deal with Its Impulses," *Pacific Standard*, Sept 15, 2014

114   The Nielsen Total Audience Report, 1st Q 2016, http://www.nielsen.com/us/en/insights/reports/2016/the-total-audience-report-q1-2016.html

115   Lynn Yaeger, "Chanel, H&M, Macy's, Diet Coke: What Should Karl Lagerfeld Design Next?" *Vogue*, August 4, 2011

116   "Are Leggings Pants," The Tylt, https://thetylt.com/culture/are-leggings-pants

117   Erin McKelle, "9 Things Women Who Wear Leggings as Pants are Tired of Hearing," *Bustle*, Mar 19, 2015

118   Chris Weller, "Japan is facing a 'death by overwork' problem – here's what it's all about," *Business Insider*, Oct 18, 2017

119   Mari Yamaguchi, "Japan overwork deaths among young show lessons unlearned," Associated Press, Oct 21, 2016

120   Brigid Schulte, "US productivity: Putting in all those hours doesn't matter," *The Washington Post*, May 14, 2014

121   *Family Guy*, Season 4, Episode 5, "The Cleveland-Loretta Quagmire"

122   Love Bites Radio Episode 70, "Be Your Most Extreme You . . . In Moderation," Heritage Radio Network, Apr 10, 2017

123   Google Dictionary

124   Claudia Wallis, "The Science of Happiness Turns 10. What Has It Taught?" *Time*, Jul 08, 2009

125   Lyubomirsky, Sonja, René M Dickerhoof, Julia K Boehm and Kennon M Sheldon. "Becoming happier takes both a will and a proper way: an experimental longitudinal intervention to boost well-being," *Emotion*, 11 2 (2011): 391–402.

126   Tim Kasser, *The High Price of Materialism*, MIT Press, 2002, Ch 3

127   Ed Diener, Martin E.P. Seligman, "Very Happy People," *Psychological Science* 2002

128   Alex Billington, "Interview: 'About Time' Writer & Director Richard Curtis on Happiness," http://www.firstshowing.net/2013/interview-about-time-writer-director-richard-curtis-on-happiness/, Nov 12, 2013

129   Kathleen D. Vohs, Joseph P. Redden, Ryan Rahinel, "Physical Order Produces Healthy Choices, Generosity, and Conventionality, Whereas Disorder Produces Creativity," *Psychological Science*, Aug 1, 2013, Vol 24, Issue 9, pp 1860–1867, https://doi.org/10.1177/0956797613480186

130   Swami Satchidananda Saraswati, Integral Yoga Teachers Association Newsletter, Vol X No. 2, May 2004

131   *Love Actually*, written and directed by Richard Curtis, 2003, Universal Pictures

132   Robb B. Rutledge et al., "Risk Taking for Potential Reward Decreases across the Lifespan," *Current Biology*, June 2016, doi: 10.1016/j.cub.2016.05.017

133   Montague confirms by email the conversation with Roko Belic as truth, but doesn't expand. People are busy.

134   Carrie Fisher, *Wishful Drinking*, Simon & Shuster, 2008

135   Tim Kasser, The High Price of Materialism, MIT Press, 2002

136   Tim Kasser references Grube JW, Mayton DM, and Ball-Rokeach SJ," Inducing Change in Values, Attitudes, and Behaviors: Belief System Theory and the Method of Value Self-Confrontation," *Journal of Social Issues*, 1994;50:153–173, doi:10.1111/j.1540-4560.1994.tb01202.x; Rokeach M, "Long-range experimental modification of values, attitudes, and behavior," *American Psychologist*, 1971;26(5):453–459; and Norman A. Polansky, *Beliefs, Attitude and Values: A Theory of Organization and Change*, Milton Rokeach, San Francisco: Jossey-Bass, 1968 *Social Work*, Volume 14, Issue 4, 1 October 1969, pp 115–116, https://doi.org/10.1093/sw/14.4.115. I read this in Kasser's *The High Price of Materialism*, MIT Press, 2002, Ch 9.

137   *About Time*, written and directed by Richard Curtis, 2013, Universal Pictures